Synthesis Lectures on Threatcasting

Series Editors

Brian David Johnson, Arizona State University, Tempe, USA

Natalie Vanatta, United States Military Academy, West Point, USA

This series publishes short books that explore the analytical method of threatcasting, which draws on a wide range of fields to develop techniques for recognizing future threats, designing potential futures, and exposing events that could indicate the progression toward an increasingly possible threat landscape. Books in this series will cover all aspects of the threatcasting methodology for researchers and practitioners. The series will promote new dialogues across a variety of communities and keep up to date with novel developments in the area.

Christopher Owens

Storycasting

Making Plausible Futures Compelling Through Speculative Fiction

 Springer

Christopher Owens
United States Secret Service
Odenton, MD, USA

ISSN 2771-1560　　　　　　ISSN 2771-1579 (electronic)
Synthesis Lectures on Threatcasting
ISBN 978-3-031-95063-6　　　ISBN 978-3-031-95064-3 (eBook)
https://doi.org/10.1007/978-3-031-95064-3

© The Editor(s) (if applicable) and The Author(s), under exclusive license to Springer Nature Switzerland AG 2026

This work is subject to copyright. All rights are solely and exclusively licensed by the Publisher, whether the whole or part of the material is concerned, specifically the rights of translation, reprinting, reuse of illustrations, recitation, broadcasting, reproduction on microfilms or in any other physical way, and transmission or information storage and retrieval, electronic adaptation, computer software, or by similar or dissimilar methodology now known or hereafter developed.
The use of general descriptive names, registered names, trademarks, service marks, etc. in this publication does not imply, even in the absence of a specific statement, that such names are exempt from the relevant protective laws and regulations and therefore free for general use.
The publisher, the authors and the editors are safe to assume that the advice and information in this book are believed to be true and accurate at the date of publication. Neither the publisher nor the authors or the editors give a warranty, expressed or implied, with respect to the material contained herein or for any errors or omissions that may have been made. The publisher remains neutral with regard to jurisdictional claims in published maps and institutional affiliations.

This Springer imprint is published by the registered company Springer Nature Switzerland AG
The registered company address is: Gewerbestrasse 11, 6330 Cham, Switzerland

If disposing of this product, please recycle the paper.

Foreword

Storytelling is a powerful tool that allows leaders to inspire, motivate, and connect with their teams by sharing compelling narratives that evoke emotions and build trust. Social media emphasizes sound bites over details and punchlines over paragraphs, and this isn't sufficient to connect to the important narratives—those that resonate with one's identity. As consumers of vast quantities of information, we are drawn to stories that capture our attention and inspire us to act. Most often, this inspiration comes when the stories resonate with *who we are*.

Threatcasting, as a systems-based planning method, sets itself apart from other scenario analysis methods, because it centers the process on people. It identifies specific actions, indicators, and concrete steps that can be taken to disrupt, mitigate, and recover from potential future threats. It leverages inputs from social science, technical research, cultural history, economics, trends, and expert interviews. The nuanced outputs are sensitive to the complexity that comes from human-centric design. These outputs are built through a structured process that encourages participants—both subject matter experts and practitioners with 'skin in the game'—to craft imaginative and collaborative discussions about unique visions of the future.

It is not uncommon for workshop outputs to include a summary, which may include an academic report, policy implications, recommendations, or other creative formats. Participants may return to their workplaces with some high-level summary, but not yet know how to communicate the workshop's importance to their organization. This is where Storycasting shines.

Understandably, Storycasting is a portmanteau—a blended word—of *storytelling* and *Threatcasting*. In Storycasting we suggest that a variety of formats are needed to help us understand these unique visions of the future. Storycasting is not a summary of findings, but rather an ongoing experiment in which readers are encouraged to participate with their own contributions. This book will give you an in-depth view of many different Storycasting formats that appeal to different audiences and communicate visions of the future in unique and compelling ways.

Cannon Beach, OR, USA   Brian David Johnson

How to Use this Book

As a part of the Threatcasting Lecture Series, *Storycasting* demonstrates how stakeholders, facilitators, post-workshop analyst teams, and participants of strategic futures workshops can present the most plausible findings into compelling formats. This book provides a brief explanation of the Threatcasting process, but it does not include an extensive background behind the methodology.

This textbook provides what the author has found to be an efficient method of converting qualitative data from a standardized model into a compelling narrative that can illicit reactions from intended audiences—in this case, senior leaders and decision makers. While the Storycasting process outlined within these pages applies data collected in a Threatcasting effort, there are other models, processes, and workshops that could also provide sufficient qualitative data to produce similar narrative outputs.

The process of *Storycasting* as demonstrated within this text is approached as an ongoing course of discovery and experimentation. It is not presented as the highest realization of the concept, but a place where others can start their own efforts to capture the attention—or inspire action—of others. Readers are encouraged to learn the concepts and steps found within this book and explore other ways to compelling present strategic thinking, conceptual future scenarios, and anticipatory thinking to all levels of their organization's decision makers.

Contents

1 **Introduction** 1
   1.1 The Folly of Expectancy 1
   1.2 Making the Plausible into the Compelling 3
   1.3 Methodology Supports Plausibility 6
   1.4 The STEEPLE Acronym 8
   1.5 Scenario-Based Planning 10
   1.6 Applying STEEPLE to Storytelling 12
   1.7 Futures Are not Predictive 17
   References 17

2 **Strategic Planning Challenges and Opportunities** 19
   2.1 Why Strategic Planning Can Fail 21
   2.2 Challenge: Resistance or Apprehension 22
   2.3 Challenge: Lack of Explicitness to the Organization 23
   2.4 Challenge: Employee Disengagement 24
   2.5 Challenge: Misunderstanding the Internal Culture 24
   2.6 Opportunity in Story Casting: Everyone Is a Participant or Contributor ... 26
   2.7 Opportunity in Storycasting: Storytelling as a Leadership Skill 27
   References 32

3 **Making It Compelling** 33
   3.1 From Bullets to Believing 34
   3.2 Public Sector Efforts 35
      3.2.1 Cartoons for the Greatest Generation 36
      3.2.2 Project Evergreen 36
      3.2.3 Force Design 2030 38
   3.3 Why Threatcasting? 39
   References 41

4	**Threatcasting to Storycasting—As Shown by Example**	43
	4.1 Storycasting Sample Exercise: China's Intended Future	45
	4.2 Storycasting Model: Participant Output	47
	4.3 Storycasting Model: The Three-Act Play	51
	4.4 Inserting Participant Responses into the Three-Act Play Template	53
	4.5 Storycasting Model: A Compelling Story	57
	4.6 Grounding Storycasting with Research	76
	References	78
5	**Other Ways to Tell a Story**	81
	5.1 Story Length	82
	5.2 Newspaper Front Pages	83
	5.3 Internal or Organization-Specific Documents	85
	5.4 Industry, Trade, or Academic Periodicals	86
	5.5 Genre Decisions	89
	5.6 Leveraging Artificial Intelligence	90
	References	93
6	**The Future of Storycasting as Viewed by the Author**	95
	Reference	97
Terms as Used in this Textbook		99

Introduction 1

1.1 The Folly of Expectancy

There was a particular day I first seriously contemplated the difference between *'having enough information to do the job'* and *'having all the information needed to excel at the mission.'* As though I was conscious about not just decision making, but the meaning and contextualization of information in an operational sense.

It was during one of many sorties I'd flown on one of many deployments I would make which was one of hundreds flown each year by many crews and planes. I was a Sensor System Operator (SSO) on an HU-25C surveillance aircraft. Our mission that day was to locate small sailboats—departing from Haiti's 'North Claw' to be exact—and interdict the ones overloaded with potential illegal migrants. Countless small wooden sailboats move up and down the Old Bahama Channel and the clusters of islands that stretch from Turks and Caicos all the way to Grand Bahama, a stone's throw from Florida's east coast. Even in calm seas, some of these boats appear to be barely afloat. We knew passengers crammed themselves into the boat's tiny cabin (if there is one) or cover themselves with tarps when planes or ships approach. It is the traditional cat-and-mouse game, and we're all playing our parts.

Two pilots up front and two people seated at large windows on both sides of the jet scanned with their naked eyes or, at night, with night-vision goggles. As the fifth member of the crew, the SSO, it was my job to operate the suite of integrated technologies. A turret resembling a beach ball on the aircraft's belly housed a dual infrared and digital camera systems that could be paired with the nose-mounted air and surface radar. Data from both systems was represented on a digital mapping system at my crew position. This allowed for tracking multiple targets and even relocating them on later sorties by extrapolating future estimated positions off their last known position (LKP). The rate of migration ebbs and flows for various reasons. The time of year, maybe? Or because something has changed the backdrop of Haiti or the Caribbean. Sometimes changes occurred for reasons we struggled to understand in the relatively short time of our deployments.

In just three days of that particular deployment, using the cameras and radar, I'd found enough dangerously overloaded boats to fill the flight deck of a ship with people that were otherwise destined to drown. Each time, we'd direct the same ship to each sailboat for intercept. Our success, in fact, required another ship to be diverted into the area while the first one proceeded south to initiate the repatriation process of the people rescued at sea.

As it tends to happen in the Caribbean, strong squalls began rolling through the area during our first sortie one morning. It was decided we'd suspend our search because the weather was no longer optimal for northerly migration via sailboat through the Old Bahama Channel.

> **Decision Point:**
>
> Question: When weather is bad for northbound sailing, what is the best course of action if you're searching for sailboats along their traditional routes?
>
> Answer: We left the search area, flew back to Guantanamo Bay, Cuba, and prepped to launch again when the weather passed.

At some point I silently wondered how migrant interdiction decisions were based on our (meaning the broader organization or specific flight crews) routine behaviors and assumptions. Not the migrant's behaviors and assumption, mind you, but again, ours.

How much of what we did in this deployment was based on our routine patterns?
How much of our decision making was based on static, not dynamic, trends?
Was something novel (new, unrealized, or innovative) influencing what was happening in that small patch of ocean?

Finding migrants was a challenge, and I wanted to know if *understanding more* could make us more effective. This type of questioning does not usually come from the technician sitting in all the way in the back of the plane. Though I'm sure any conversation with the rest of the crew would have been amicable, had I asked any of these questions, they would probably be politely dismissed as pedantic. Nevertheless, the next day we flew again as did hundreds of other sorties that year. The routines of Caribbean migrant deployments continue to this day, though I have not been a part of them in over a decade and things have likely changed since my description.

After retiring from active duty in 2012, I studied International Relations and then completed a graduate program in International Development and Social Change. I devoured courses on qualitative research, sociology, development strategies, organizational behavior, and all manners of gap and needs analysis. My capstone was, not surprisingly, a study on the intersection of refugee policy and ongoing trends in human long-term mobility and migration—also called protracted displacement (see note). I wanted to answer, with academic rigor, some of the many unanswered questions I had while flying through the Caribbean years earlier. Not just about weather and sailboats, but about the deeper issues behind human migration movements.

Fast forward and I find myself leveraging qualitative research methods, gap analysis, and deep research as an analyst in various capacities. By this writing, I have spent nearly two decades as an analyst. First, in organizational behavior and process improvement while on active duty. Later, I honed my craft by conducting training assessments, job task analyses, human performance assessments and strategic planning and assessing emerging technical capabilities. Always however, with a sociologist's eye and a seemingly endless list of questions.

> Note: The Office of the United Nations High Commissioner for Refugees (UNHCR) defines a protracted refugee situation as one in which 25,000 or more refugees from the same nationality have been in exile for five or more years in a given asylum country. UNHCR estimates that the average length of major protracted refugee situations has risen to 26 years.

1.2 Making the Plausible into the Compelling

A few years ago, while participating in an analysis and writing team, we were looking through outputs from a Threatcasting workshop. Threatcasting, as it will be better explained later, is strategic foresight methodology and framework that brings together multidisciplinary groups in a guided workshop format. During the workshop, participants often formed into cohorts working collaboratively, envision trends that could become **threats** to their industry in the future.

At one particular point, possibly my fourth opportunity as either a participant, analyst, or writer, I found myself looking at the qualitative data being created and saw it with a different lens. As with previous Threatcasting efforts, each cohort produced two or three unique scenarios: different crimes, victims, methodologies, and locations. What was produced in the end was a substantial spreadsheet of data for each scenario—over thirty scenarios in total. We summarized the meaning of each scenario and then, through iterations, isolated the novelty of the threat or risk; what was new or could be unrealized until after it is enacted. We looked for futures scenarios that represented the most salient points we would include in the final report. Because the Threatcasting methodology requires participants to start with *a person*, we always felt like we knew the victim or protagonist and the threat they faced. What I saw differently was that I wanted to show the data differently. Not change it, mind you, but make something new and greater out of it.

A few of the cohorts had time to add more complexity or interesting details to the antagonists. For instance, they didn't just have 'the bad actor' or a faceless organization or just listed 'state-sponsored criminal organization,' but they gave them more compelling backstories. Unlike most Bond villains, their motives were more than just 'make crime.' We could understand why the bad actor or bad actors engaged in criminal behavior.

The victim in these scenarios was not just a random name with a non-descript job occupation, but it was a person—or people—in a situation with which the sponsor or stakeholder of the project could empathize. Maybe they lived like any other person and relied on the same technology or financial systems. They could be in their same social class. Or a character emulated a relative of theirs. They are retired just like a neighbor, or worked in an industry, or they were in a high school like one of your employees' children. The characters in some of these scenarios sounded like someone with whom the stakeholder could easily relate. Or they sounded just like… you. Or me. Or someone we know in our organization.

They did not create a full story, per se, but they built the framework for one. What futurist and author Alvin Toffler would call a *simulated environment,* not just an imaginary world. The participants created a complete skeleton, with all the bones in all the right places. Toffler described an ideal next step. All that was needed was the skin and tissue attached to the skeleton, and we would have a "work of art into which the audience may actually walk, and inside which things happen" [1]. The scenarios provided more than enough information to build a plot. Enough to write a short story.

This collection of data from the workshops was the inspiration for Storycasting—before the new word even came to mind. With no resistance from the rest of the Threatcasting analysis and writing team, I took one of the more robust scenarios and converted it into text of a fictitious news report taking place ten years in future; something more readable than an efficient list of bullet points and more absorbing than a spreadsheet. Even though it was written in the format of exposition like a news article and without any character dialogue, it became three-dimensional and closer to that *simulated environment*, Toffler described.

A few weeks later, using the information another cohort created, I drafted a simulated newspaper article. I chose the scenario carefully as I needed one that was fully formed and was rich with details—the bones from which to create flesh and sinew. One in particular jumped out from the others. It outlined a false flag shooting in a Toronto School. The main character was not just the antagonist, but a form of victim themselves. I used the information to create a news article placed ten years in the future. The news article ended with unanswered questions about who committed the crime and why. After the text of the news article was complete, it needed just few images from the Internet of police cruisers, children filing out of an elementary school, a person under arrest, and frightened teachers.

1.2 Making the Plausible into the Compelling

Then I created some quotes from one or two of the characters and polished it off with some colorful journalistic-ish formatting (see Fig. 1.1).

Departing Lead Investigator describes surreal moments during year-long investigation in school shooting hoax.

The Proverbial Press
October 3, 2030
Written by: Bernard Webber

Investigator says the team of 20 experienced a "double reality" that was unlike anything they had encountered.

This week marks the one-year anniversary of the oddest act of domestic terrorism in Canada. Lead investigator Guy Massa leaves the case bewildered, exhausted, and holding only a partial understanding of what occurred. His final report is being released to the public on Monday, however it promises to leave the international coalition of federal investigators feeling unfulfilled.

At 9:46 am on September 3rd last year, Toronto Police began receiving calls from different numbers, all reporting an active shooter had entered the Lawrence Park North Elementary School, many confirming children were being shot. At roughly the same time, video images of the shooting appeared on multiple social media sites as it was happening live. Viewers were stunned as at least three of the videos seemed to come from inside classrooms and hallways of the school and others showed the frantic and chaotic evacuation of dozens of people. Graphic footage of children bleeding on the floors were paralleled by the calls to Toronto's emergency lines, where voices claiming to be teachers or students corroborated the attack. Tragically, many parents viewed the videos live and recognized their own children as some of the dead and wounded. However, when police and emergency personnel arrived on scene in full tactical gear, they found no shooter, no wounded or dead children, and no indication that anything that was being reported – and viewed live – actually occurred. First responders were met by a bewildered school staff, operating like any other day. As the day unfolded, many thought the *Twilight Zone* episode they watched had come to an end. However, Guy Massa and the team of over twenty investigators from four nations would learn, it was only Episode One of a miniseries no one ever wanted to binge.

Early investigations showed promise of a swift discovery of the truth.

Within the first three weeks, Canadian authorities identified Abed Samahd, a 23-year-old brilliant and unemployed computer science graduate from Serbian Federal University, was at the root of those disturbing and enigmatic events. During the investigation and subsequent interviews with Abed, facts became difficult to separate from fiction. The investigators were constantly amazed how the suspect always seemed to "voluntarily confess to authorities of having participated in the simulated massacre" in almost the same way as having been picked up on charges of drug possession – which he confessed to in late 2024. With virtually no effort on the investigator's part, they quickly learned that Abed, then faced with financial insecurity, agreed to taking employment through an unknown online recruiter. With no contract agreement or personal contact with anyone, he was regularly paid through direct digital deposits into his formerly empty bank accounts. For the first time in three years, Abed explained, he was "able to live my life beyond the next meal." In return, he was asked to use his exceptional skills to occasionally break the law. According to Massa, "he was assured there would be no direct threat to his life, although his risk taking this job has made him work with some questionable allies through his secondary income doing odd programming jobs for hire." While Massa's investigation found details on the 'questionable allies' he referenced, Canadian authorities have refused to provide the public any further information on who they are or how they might contribute to Abed's story. This last detail has fueled conspiracy theories.

After a few inconsequential odd jobs that involved internet searches and some "light hacking of Ontario's provincial government websites," he was asked to identify patterns of the Toronto Police and RCMP around the Lawrence Park North neighborhood. He was given a data set of police activity in the area that was posted on Kaggle by the police for a competition they ran 6 months earlier. Following the success, the same contact asked him to create two automated

Fig. 1.1 One of the author's early writing experiments creating a fictitious future news story from data collected during a Threatcasting workshop

It was no longer a list of dry imagined facts; it was a three-page news report. It was even a little uncomfortable to read. The original information was not changed; it was just as the creators of the scenario defined it. Timelines and characters and impacts were all there just as they intended. Only now, it was a *story*.

While the Threatcasting participants knew every detail that led up to the manifestation of the threat and how the victims were chosen and the techniques used in the attack, the news article was intentionally more ambiguous. It was not an After-Action Report, and it was a recounting of the event from the victims and investigators. This reflected the way a news story is often presented—a series of developing details and uncorroborated facts. It left the reader unsure of what happened. It included contradicting accounts of the event and even opposing views of who conducted the attack. It reflected how we get our news: in an imperfect manner. That too, made it feel real.

In just a few hours of work, the details of their scenario became a story that could illicit not just consideration, but a reaction from the reader. It was an experiment and did not include fully developed graphics or layout, but it was enough to consider that *storytelling* was a more compelling way to present a plausible future scenario than a dry list of information.

I shared it with the rest of the team and ideas started bouncing around as we looked at other scenarios cohorts put together. We could not use the fictitious news article in the final report, but I felt I was on to something. It certainly wasn't new, but a reimagining of a familiar idea. More questions fueled more ideas.

Would the details in another scenario be thought-provoking if they were part of an internal corporate presentation? What are the implications to the private sector?

What if we took another one and wrote it as a high-level briefing to senior leadership (a mayor, governor, police chief, head of emergency management, or military general) where senior officers have opinions and opposing priorities?

Do we think that one of them might have enough detail to become a short story?

1.3 Methodology Supports Plausibility

> "You can't connect the dots looking forward; you can only connect them looking backwards. So you have to trust that the dots will somehow connect in your future." Steve Jobs.

Analysts frequently ask a fair amount of *Why?* and *How?* questions. We also like *For how long?* and *Who else?* and an occasional *Where would we see that happen?* and *What else could this impact?* These sometimes appear beyond the scope of any project in front of us. That is because people who work in strategic foresight planning, especially, are drawn to the minutia as well as the major changes in an issue. We consider the **spurious**

1.3 Methodology Supports Plausibility

relationships between issues. Researching news articles and attending panel discussions helps understand broad environments and discrete signals, a key element to strategic foresight planning. Working in this domain often means building plausible futures scenarios based on multiple potential courses of ongoing trends. Studying those trends means going back through the history of an issue, building an understanding of it, and then extrapolate how that trend might continue, or change based on intersections and interactions of other trends.

There are many foresight options out there. Many models are accessible through training sessions, hiring an external consultancy, or purchasing access to a proprietary model. Regardless, any strategic foresight effort—when done with intended deliverables—encourages organizations to take a comprehensive view of potential opportunities and threats with a broader and longer-term perspective. It involves an outside-in approach, utilizing various methods to grasp future trends and envision multiple potential futures.

Strategic foresight should go well beyond the immediate concerns of an organization. Prompting them to consider societal and political shifts, application(s) of emerging technologies, and innovations in related industries. While these signals of change may seem distant or irrelevant initially, they have the potential to trigger disruptive transformations that will influence the future direction of the organization.

For instance, a pharmaceutical company may use this type of thinking—sometimes called **competitive intelligence**—to monitor current developments in drug patents, regulatory changes, and competitor actions. However, their strategic foresight team would also analyze broader, long-term trends in technology, societal attitudes, and cultural shifts—such as the rise of personalized medicine or the impact of social media misinformation or public trust in healthcare—to anticipate how these factors could shape the industry landscape in the coming years.

Therefore, the goal of strategic foresight is not only to track these diverse signals of change but to integrate them into a cohesive narrative. This is a complex task as there is no single definitive future outcome but rather one that provides the reader some ability to anticipate threats and opportunities to come. However, by developing compelling scenarios of multiple potential futures, strategic foresight enables organizations to create adaptable and resilient strategies that can navigate and capitalize on the unpredictable.

Following a structured process will guide participants to think about the potential evolution of trends in a methodological way. It will help keep the process focused yet still open-ended enough, nurturing creative thinking and innovative ideas. It will also ensure that the internal logic of scenario descriptions is consistent and linked to concrete business opportunities and plausible threats. And this effort traditionally includes the exploration of *multiple* potential futures, not just a pair of most desired or least desired—or 'what we want' versus 'what we don't want.' One way you can tell that your plausible futures are reaching far enough is when you start to feel yourself saying "That would never happen." Do not fear that moment. Rather, trust that this feeling is letting you know your efforts are yielding something *compelling*. One of the earliest and well-respected writers on the subject, Jim Dator, provided us with one of the most basic guidelines in that "any useful statement about the future should at first seem ridiculous" [2].

1.4 The STEEPLE Acronym

Foresight and scenario-based planning models develop plausible future scenarios using the relationship of multiple **critical uncertainties**. This task does not foretell a certain future but rather map out plausible futures. Then an organization can build resilience, by proposing '*If this future—or one like it—were to come to fruition, what opportunities or risks would develop?*' But with so many critical uncertainties, it is helpful to provide some contextual groupings early in the process.

Using a STEEPLE analysis—an extension of the lesser comprehensive PESTEL analysis—helps frame or contextualize the breadth of external factors affecting a business. The acronym STEEPLE represents six categories or themes to analyze areas of future opportunity or threats to an organization or industry, to include Social, Technological, Economic, Environmental, Political, Legal, and Ethical factors. Adherents to PESTLE often omit the ethical category, including those ideas in either the social or political grouping. By assessing these themes—or critical uncertainties—a foresight project can gain insights that guide strategic decision-making, risk assessment, and long-term planning.

The STEEPLE Acronym Can Lead to Informative Questions

> **Social (S)**—What movements in society or culture are providing push-and-pull? Internal to our organization or external to our customer?
> **Technological (T)**—What are the developing tools and innovations? What is their application—intended or unintended?
> **Economic (E)**—What are the financial influences? Where are gains or losses?
> **Environmental (E)**—In what ways can ecological changes provide opportunities or increase risk? Often, health is included in this topic.
> **Political (P)**—How are public affairs and governance included or influenced? May include local, national, or international as appropriate.
> **Legal (L)**—What laws or authorities are applicable? How are they applied or circumvented?
> **Ethical (E)**—How is 'right' or moral determined? By whom is it determined?

Some foresight planning models develop plausible future scenarios using the relationship, or intersection of two trends, and others intentionally include an examination of all at the same time. Again, the goal is to extrapolate each of these trends into assumed or predetermined future date. Author of *4 Steps to the Future*, Richard Lum—and many others—points out that a **trend** is "a historical change over time" [3]. This task does

1.4 The STEEPLE Acronym

not portend a certain future but rather map out plausible future trends—or **critical uncertainties**.

Many strategic planning models start by developing a set of critical uncertainties that fall into STEEPLE categories. For instance, a global clothing brand might want to explore the future of their industry by focusing on trends or uncertainties specific to them.

> **Supply Chain Stability** could reflect anticipated trends in the economy (E) or the environment (E).
> **Consumer Adoption of Digital Currency** could be contextualized as either a social (S), or economic (E) trend.
> **Fashion Periodical Formats** may represent a technological (T) trend.
> **Social Media Influencers** might reflect either social trends (S) or even reflect the ethical changes (E) seen in fashion.
> **Impact of International Tariffs** would help develop economic (E) or political (P) influences.
> **Market Share of Knockoffs** in the fashion manufacturing industry might reflect economic or ethical (E) factors or regulatory policies (P).

These ideas would vary depending on the intent of the strategic futures effort; however, the focus should have the identical predetermined point in the future, not simply current threats versus opportunities. The poles or extremes of those uncertainties would also be defined. These poles or extremes help define the perceived limits of changes in any change. While it is most likely that a future state would be someplace in the middle, it helps to define those boundaries. This can be subjective; however, it will help create limits.

> **Supply Chain Stability** could be 'high' versus 'low' or 'stable' or 'dynamic' depending on the intended context.
> **Consumer Adoption of Digital Currency** could be 'ubiquitous' or 'atypical.'
> **Fashion Periodical Formats** could be 'print only' versus 'digital only.'
> **Social Media Influencers** could be 'supportive' or 'derogatory.'
> **Impact of International Tariffs** could be 'export favoring' or 'import favoring.'
> **Market Share of Knockoffs** could be 'predatory' or 'ineffective.'

The extremes would be characterized based on a level of threat or opportunity to your industry or company. Then an organization can build resilience, by proposing "If this future—or one like it—were to come to fruition, what opportunities or threat would develop?" Threats are things for which we have some sort of data or even a perception or sense of 'what could be' based on what we know, "from which we produce the trend lines of graphs" [4].

A quick note about perspective here—and will be covered more later—a broad viewpoint from within an organization would be most beneficial in building both the agreed-upon trends and the definition of their poles or extremes. Limiting this examination of trends to a small portion of the organization—in this case, only a sales department or shipping department—would limit the perspective and impacts to only those elements of the business. Prior to beginning any foresight or futures effort, the scope and perspective should be defined. This provides the facilitators and participants with refined goals and limits by which to operate.

1.5 Scenario-Based Planning

Scenario-based planning (sometimes annotated as SBP) serves as a methodology that embraces multiple uncertainties of the future as its foundation. This requires a methodical imagination. By combining subject matter knowledge with a healthy dose of intuitive logic, scenarios provide well-founded yet imaginative depictions of potential futures. It creates high-level narratives to make the outcomes of foresight work more interesting not only for the participants in the process, but also for the recipients of the outputs. For this and all-other circumstances in this book, we will consider the final recipient either a senior executive, a senior decision maker, or groups of either or both.

The process begins by defining a research question or determining how the outputs of the effort will be used. For many, the natural end-results are recommendations to an organization's long-term strategic goals or risk metrics. Describe the main themes, topics, or key 'what if' questions you want to explore. To further narrow down your scope, also determine the year when your scenarios will be taking place. Participants then conduct a thorough scan for trends or critical uncertainties that are pertinent to your organization. Some efforts also include concepts like megatrends, wild cards, or weak signals of change, to a comprehensive and diverse set of trends that represent all of the STEEPLE categories. **Stakeholders** are traditionally asked to narrow the list of uncertainties, either as a vote or prioritization according to specified criteria (e.g., the level of uncertainty and threat) to prioritize key uncertainties regarding the specific point in the future.

Next, the effort includes forming an intersection of two trends or critical uncertainties from the agreed-upon STEEPLE categories. Placing two uncertainties in a 2×2 matrix creates four potential future scenarios with differing characteristics where the participants consider the threats and opportunities that might reside in each (see Fig. 1.2). Participants give each scenario a title and maintain narratives rich with multiple perspectives and actionable insights [5]. Some efforts take the added challenge of intersection three uncertainties and create a three-dimensional cube with eight potential future **plausible futures**.

The scenario-based planning model is easily repeatable and effective in identifying broad ideas useful to build general resilience and preparation—not specific strategies or

1.5 Scenario-Based Planning

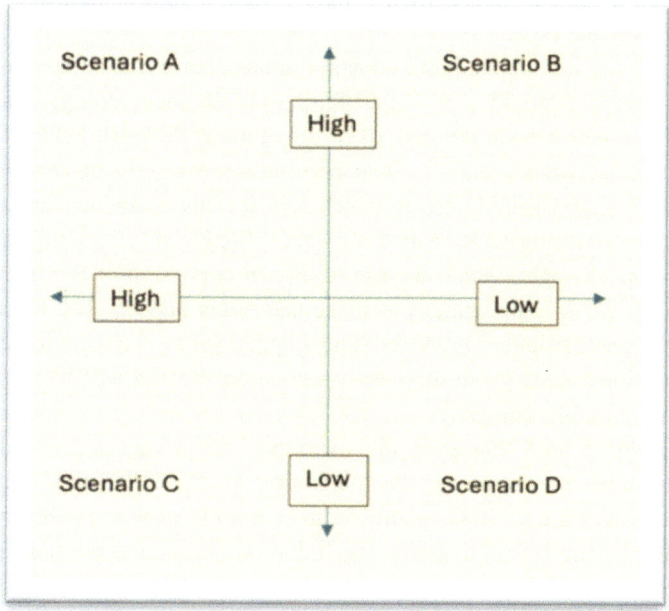

Fig. 1.2 Scenario-based planning matrix as described by the author

interventions. By design, they only apply at the upper echelon—an industry view, organizational view, or possibly the view of department or segment of an organization. For anything more compelling, say a fully developed vignette, scenario-based planning can provide 'the world in the future' but not the characters who live in that future. However, there are some successes that will be discussed later.

Admittedly, I am dubious of scenario-based planning efforts that also demand participants or stakeholders select futures that fit a perception that one of these multiple futures is preferred over the other. Some efforts insist that a rank order is applied potential futures from best to worst. Though there is a historical criterion for this. Jim Dator wrote a set of four archetypes he defined as *growth, constraint, collapse,* and *transformation* [6]. The risk applying this to a scenario-based planning 2×2 grid is that we can find ourselves intentionally selecting—and even ranking—four potential futures based on an assumed taxonomy before we determine what threats and opportunities each future will hold. We can lose our **objectivity** about a future when we do this.

It can be tempting to perceive a future in which funding, for instance, is preferred to be 'high' versus 'low.' However, that assumes that financial windfalls do not bring as many pressures or threats (irresponsible spending or an influx of public or political scrutiny) as they do opportunities. Or that the economic impact of a preferred or ideal trend should be 'carbon neutral' versus 'increased pollutant' without first considering the economic burden of one over the other.

Yes, it is tempting to imagine best and worst futures, but if that is the mindset we apply to the future, then you should also—in all fairness to the methodology—determine what *present* we are in had it been defined 10 or 20 years in the past. What 'future' are we living in now? To accurately classify your present as either *growth, constraint, collapse,* and *transformation,* you would need to benchmark it to the same distant past that we are building our potential futures. Richard Lum states "Reduced to its simplest formulation, we try to develop foresight, which we use to inform our vision of the future we want to achieve, and then we develop strategy to make that future happen" [7]. He is not insisting we focus on the one particular, preferred, and singular future we want to achieve. Rather, we want to develop a strategy so that our organization's vision will be responsive to *any* of the countless possible futures.

It is important to note that even in government or private sector industries where security implications are germane, the integration of STEEPLE trends collected from Open-Source Intelligence (OSINT) sources can be used to explore resiliency in long-term strategic planning. The key is to frame the initial questions and problem in such a way that the data collected is broad enough to capture generalized trends yet still focused to provide meaningful results.

1.6 Applying STEEPLE to Storytelling

An early experiment with storytelling involved me scanning news articles, journal and academic reports, and other publicly available sources to answer a series of questions. Intentionally and systematically replacing "that is implausible" and instead embracing "what implications might we see" allows for free-thinking. What novel applications of artificial intelligence (AI) and machine learning (ML) look like in the food industry?

> What tangential impacts would influence this, and what would these novel applications influence?
> Using STEEPLE as a framework, how complex and plausible would this appear as a news article in the future?

Removing any needless distractions of visual appearance or layout, I spent a few weeks in early 2022 gathering information and synthesizing it into an imagined future state. With nothing but the Internet, STEEPLE, and the above framing or scoping questions to guide me, the content slowly transitioned from plausible to compelling. In the end I created a

1.6 Applying STEEPLE to Storytelling

simulated article downloaded from the fictitious website foodsecurity.org on October 13, 2035.

Despite National Food Shortages, One State Becomes the Unwitting Center of AI Angst.

Last week, Texas formalized into law a sweeping requirement that 65% of food production conducted by any farm, company, or small business must be accomplished by human workers. In doing so, Texas joins other states in regulating AI in food production, but unlike other states, Texas has unfairly become the social media focal point for a complex issue.

Some states, like Alabama on the other hand, have strategically made no such regulation. For the past ten years companies that use up to 100% AI and robotic technology in their processing have been migrating to Alabama and similar states in anticipation of these regulations. Based on policy and business trends of the last decade, industry leaders and economists anticipate the growing fissure between employment and efficiency will spread to other domains.

Banning together in 2027, eight states including Texas, made an initial anti-automation stance by passing some version of Work Safety Program Regulations (WSPR)—sarcastically called 'whisper laws' on social media posts that claim they were passed through corporate pressures and are only 'soft restrictions.' WSPRs hyper-tax the import of "non-compliant food production" from any other state. WSPR regulations were created before AI-driven food production took hold anywhere in the US. As AI developed, so did the language in various regulations. For instance, some state WSPR regulations require extra inspections for AI-produced food. Corporations complain that states have been known to delay inspections to intentionally disrupt supply chains and even spoil fresh food.

The US has long been a leader in AI and robotics development; however, the use of non-human production work has created one more split between federal and state interests. It is no surprise that competing ideologies are fought in legislative chambers. "Lawmakers have been creating a legislative battlefront along state lines for years," says professor and economist John Fernando, "and here we see laws that may shield states from less-than-desirable federal initiatives. In this case, however, national food security is impacted."

The largest company to move into a friendlier area was Kerry Foods, who previously converted their $2.1B San Antonio canning production line to AI-powered analytics and robotics. Aside from physically unloading trucks of product by hand, vegetables were sorted, inspected, trimmed, cleaned, re-inspected, and packaged by smart-tech machines that troubleshoot and monitor production at incredibly high speed—faster and more accurately than humans. Citing increasing financial hurdles in San Antonio, Kerry Foods invested billions to relocate and took with them millions of dollars of state tax revenue when they moved to nearby Arkansas. Since the move, their distribution and sales beat competitors with ease.

Texas voters have been the most vocal, executing social media campaigns shared around the world. The state has been the 'canary in the coalmine,' demonstrating how states will continue to suffer food shortages while the food production industries slowly migrate to states that adopt Nutrition Innovation Subsidy Programs (NISP). NISP regulations provide financial incentives to companies that develop carbon-responsible processes and lower human injuries by rolling out robotics and AI-driven automation in the most hazardous areas of production. Economists agree that by the end of 2035, food prices are predicted to skyrocket out of control in affected regions of the US, while food prices will remain stable or drop elsewhere.

At the 2028 "4M Fisheries Conference" seafood manufacturers from Maine, Mississippi, Massachusetts, and Maryland considered lobbying for similar laws related to coastal and deep-sea fishing and shellfish. As countries like China and North Korea continually add AI technologies to their global (and illegal) fishing fleets, American seafood companies are falling behind. Citing privately funded research by universities, they determined the marriage of AI and robotics applications rarely impact employment rates. Industry and state leaders reached compromises; their regulations now apply only to shore-side processing and packaging facilities. So as early adopters of automation in those states watched unemployment rise, the displaced workforce was absorbed by other waterfront industries or by worker migration to other areas of the US.

This is not solely an American issue. European nations like France, Germany, and Spain have adopted national agricultural and meat processing automation without regional polarizing regulations. Removing humans from direct contact with pesticides in fields and animal bodily fluids, it is argued, lowers risk of birth defects and transmission of viruses between animals and humans. EU health ministers and WHO support this through decades of data from multiple research findings across the globe. Citing 2020 COVID mutations in Denmark mink farms and the rapid 2026 mutation of viruses in meat processing plants in the US, Brazil, and France, NSIP laws are designed to help people, not hurt them, it is argued.

The rise of AI is an economic opportunity for some companies. Monsanto, for instance, once the unloved poster child of poisonous agriculture across Europe, is now expanding sales in nations that promote robotic farming, thereby making pesticides less of a threat to the health of field workers. US states and other nations that promote WSPR initiatives claim that the widespread automation of physical labor

1.6 Applying STEEPLE to Storytelling

in the production of food is symptomatic of societies that, according to a TikTok posting that reached over 2 billion shares, "abdicate regulators from promoting safe food" and "allow humans to be distanced from the realities of industrial meat and poultry production." Prominent political and religious leaders around the globe have been critical of the replacement of humans—and by extension, our humanity—by AI and automation.

It was a surprise to many when Pope Hubert joined an international consortium of writers, social movement leaders, and various retired politicians to speak out about the immorality and inhumanity of relying on machines to care for—and now feed—people. The world's daily awareness of failures in AI applications in French law enforcement, Israeli intelligence gathering, and Japan's hyper-advanced rail and air transportation systems only gives rise to skepticism. Public opinion provides not just a metric to measure risk or success, but as South African musician, actress, and influencer-activist Jenna G recently called the "unethical replacement of humans from nourishing humanity."

Back in the US, growing industrial automation was challenged before Congress by 15 union organizations who successfully lobbied federal lawmakers to ban automated shipping on all interstate highways and railways one year ago (see peoplebeforerobots.org for more). NSIP proponents agree the rise in black market food distributors, the resurgence in backyard gardening (our great-great-grandparents called it subsistence farming and our great-grandparents had Victory Gardens), online food shopping, and desperate consumers engaging in illegal border food shopping continues to weaken their stance.

The rise in illegal food trafficking into Texas from Mexico is now exacerbated into a federal law enforcement issue, drawing DC lawmakers into yet another division on the Senate and Congress floors. An unnamed source within US. Customs and Border Patrol was recently quoted on social media stating, "Black market food smuggling has been so successful that drug cartels are now diversifying their operations." He also quipped, "It's not like the old days when drug mules carried bags of cocaine instead of almonds and wheat." State and Federal governments are struggling to reach consensus on what legal authorities or agencies will enforce illegal cross-state food sales.

As Texas weathers the American public's scrutiny, the disparity between state regulations in the US is attracting attention of nations around the world as Internet outlets report competing stories from the federal, state, local, and personal narrative. Most recently, the UN High Commission on Sustainable Development released an unexpected and equally inflammatory statement comparing regional US food production shortages to what "African nations experienced in the 1980s and early 1990s." As nations like Canada, Sweden, Russia, and China prepare for their environmental summit, key financial, technical, and pharmaceutical leaders are beginning to wonder if their economic partnerships with the US will be pressured by this emerging issue.

Below are online sources that influenced and informed the above fictitious article:

- Ethics of AI: https://www.nytimes.com/2020/12/03/technology/google-researcher-timnit-gebru.html
- European food production: https://ec.europa.eu/jrc/en/publication/eur-scientific-and-technical-research-reports/farmers-future
- European Medicine and AI: https://www.therobotreport.com/4-robotics-applications-accelerated-by-covid-19/
- Geopolitics of Business: https://www.economist.com/leaders/2021/06/05/the-new-geopolitics-of-global-business
- Social media: https://www.huffingtonpost.jp/entry/story_jp_5f7a68bcc5b64cf6a25235ed
- American Factories and Robots: https://www.cnn.com/2021/05/04/economy/manufacturing-jobs-economy/index.html
- Robots learning Humanity: https://www.newscientist.com/article/2275323-robot-taught-table-etiquette-can-explain-why-it-wont-follow-the-rules/
- Mink Farm: https://www.nationalgeographic.com/animals/article/what-the-mink-coronavirus-pandemic-has-taught-us
- AI and healthcare: https://www.ft.com/content/376a5494-7237-4ed6-a528-5e45712c148d
- AI and Law Enforcement: https://www.theverge.com/2021/5/21/22447446/citizen-app-internal-slack-palisades-fire-arson-bounty-manhunt-los-angeles
- AI accelerators: https://www.nextplatform.com/2021/06/24/what-happens-when-multiplication-no-longer-defines-aiaccelerators/
- Hands Free AI Farm https://interestingengineering.com/fully-automated-hands-free-farm-will-replace-workers-with-robots-and-ai
- AI Trucking https://www.reddit.com/r/SelfDrivingCars/comments/kd52n0/im_waymos_head_of_engineering_for_trucking_ama/
- AI Trucking https://www.govtech.com/fs/Curb-Management-Pilots-Smooth-the-Flow-of-Traffic-Deliveries.html
- China and global fishing: https://slate.com/news-and-politics/2020/09/beijing-fishing-fleet-subsidies-north-korea.html

1.7 Futures Are not Predictive

Before continuing, it is important to remind ourselves what strategic planning and futures work are *not*. It is not absolute. It is not **predictive**. It is not a promise. Widely accepted as one of the seminal authors on the topic, Lum reminds us that the future holds many possibilities, it does not exist until we—everyone—create it, and it is constantly in flux. It is with this understanding that strategic futures planning efforts—either as an organizational capacity or a repeated exercise—are accomplished to assist in resilience to potential emerging threats and readiness to potential emerging opportunities. In a more recent writing on the idea of foresight one author points out that her work in 2012 explored a global pandemic and admits it would have likely—and mistakenly—been seen as "wrong" had it been taken as a gospel-like prediction and applied immediately, and therefore COVID impacts would have been completely anticipated nearly a decade later. She reminds us "That's not the point—forecasts are provocations, not predictions" [8].

> Whether we call it strategic planning or strategic foresight, the idea is anticipation not precision.
> Resilience, not inoculation.
> Readiness, not percentage-of-accuracy.

Understanding how to use this information is important. The risk to drive more analysis and review into this kind of information—"Let's make sure we get it as close to perfect as possible" for instance—can derail successful implementation. If momentum is lost during strategy implementation, it is often due to reluctance or uncertainty. There is an observable impact to this error. Retired four-star general Stanley McChrystal once noted that some individuals seek to eliminate uncertainty—a byproduct of the folly of prediction—entirely by gathering more information, leading to increased hesitancy and inaction [9]. It is crucial for leaders to recognize that complete certainty is unattainable and to instead focus on taking decisive action based on the information available.

References

1. Toffler A (1970) Future shock. Bantam Books, New York
2. Bezold C. Jim Dator's alternative futures and the path to IAF's aspirational futures. Institute for Alternative Futures. Downloaded from https://jfsdigital.org/wp-content/uploads/2014/01/142-E01.pdf
3. Lum RKA (2016) 4 steps to the future. Honolulu, Futurescribe
4. Steps to the future, P17
5. Sandal G (2019, March 9) How to build scenarios efficiently with a scenario planning process. Futures Platform. Retrieved 1 May 2024, from https://www.futuresplatform.com/blog/scenario-planning-process)

6. Bezold C. Jim Dator's alternative futures and the path to IAF's aspirational futures. Institute for Alternative Futures. Downloaded from https://jfsdigital.org/wp-content/uploads/2014/01/142-E01.pdf. The abstract can be read at: https://onlinelibrary.wiley.com/https://doi.org/10.1002/ffo2.17
7. Steps to the Future, P2
8. Sha S (2022, June 24) Predictions aren't the point: lessons from forecasting the pandemic. IFTF Foresight Essentials. 13 Jul 2021. Retrieved March 15, 2024 from https://medium.com/foresight-matters/predictions-arent-the-point-lessons-from-forecasting-the-pandemic-621130de437a
9. Olson AB (2022, June 24) Common reasons strategies fail. Harvard Business Review. Retrieved March 15, 2024 from https://hbr.org/2022/06/4-common-reasons-strategies-fail

Strategic Planning Challenges and Opportunities

2

The phrase 'thinking outside the box' has aged well, but it has aged. A Wikipedia entry suggests it could date back to the 1880s. Or that it may have gained traction in the business world sometime in the 1950s. Regardless, it persists as a metaphor for that exercise where you must connect nine dots in a three-by-three grid using only four straight lines. The 'trick' is that the limit of the playing field extends beyond the confines of the three-by-three grid. Maybe it has become a cliché for having innovative solutions. Maybe it is an overused trope. Regardless, it is often used to encourage more creative thinking, limit barriers, and expand possibilities when developing strategic futures efforts (Fig. 2.1).

Consider the following real-world case study in expanding the limits of future-thinking. Place yourself in a specific moment very early in the 1990s. With America's help, a protracted and failed invasion of the sovereign nation of Afghanistan helped dismantle the Soviet Union. It seemed organizations like NATO, the World Bank, and the United Nations inched closer to long-term stabilization of global balances of power. Many leading thinkers in government and the private sector spoke as though the American preeminence was uncontestable. Many even went so far as to debate what exactly the United States should do with its enormous inheritance of power, dominance in international trade, and political influence over other nations. Trust in US power and global leadership was largely unquestioned. Without the ability to extend thinking beyond assumed confines of the contemporary balances, many national and industrial leaders were left ill-prepared for changes. Those changes spanned, of course, many of the STEEPLE categories discussed earlier.

Consider that since that moment in the early 1990s, the United States has fought multiple wars and occupied nations in the Middle East, faced an increasingly indignant Russia, an economically assertive China, and threatening nuclear weapons programs

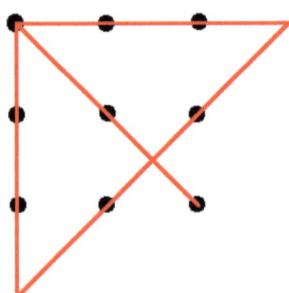

Fig. 2.1 Concept behind the phrase "Thinking Outside the Box" as described by the author. If you assume the limits of the 'playing field' are defined by the dots, you miss the opportunity to connect all nine dots with four straight lines. This is anecdotal to the idea of futures thinking. As soon as you say, "that would never happen," you have artificially limited your thinking

in North Korea and Iran. The US led the rest of the world into the Internet age where information came to everyone's fingertips. The European Union (EU) was formed and destabilization—political, economic, and social—produced multiple and persistent refugee movements. Within just the previous decade, polarized social and political movements threaten destabilization *within* the borders of many nations, including the US. An economic alliance was formed between Brazil, Russia, India, China, and South Africa (BRICS), and terms like disinformation became a part of our national vernacular.

At the time of this writing, Russia is increasingly positioned as America's international ally after they invaded another sovereign nation, BRICS membership continues to grow, artificial intelligence has transformed from science fiction to freeware, membership in the EU has been questioned, and other forms of currency—including cryptocurrency—are threatening to replace the US dollar as the global standard. As individuals, we rely on China to build our phones.

It would be hard to hypothesize most of these ideas in the 1990s. Harder still, to present them as plausible developments to a government or private sector leader back in the early 1990s. Likely most of those changes, should they be presented as possible or plausible, would be met with "That would never happen." Yet these changes came. In a later section of this textbook, reference will be made to a memo by a man named Lin Wells that aptly summarizes how foresight is a challenging effort even with the best of processes and intentions in place. Essentially, the above paragraphs should encourage—not discourage—the idea of methodical future-thinking.

Encourage imagination but define reasonable goals. The purpose of foresight and strategic planning is not simply a mental exercise or imaginative drill—though they are ingredients. It should, through a methodical approach, provide tangible and thorough outcomes that can be put to use. A view of possible threats and opportunities has already been mentioned multiple times. But what are we hoping to do with that information?

The answer will vary depending on an organization's structures and cultures, but there are solid options. As discussed in the book *Superforecasting*, restrain your reliance on probabilities for long-term planning [1]. It could provide perspective. It could challenge an organization—from the senior leaders and decision makers as well as the corps of employees—to be adaptable. It could increase the ability to scope an industry's changing landscape and increase resilience to those changes. It could provide a sense of 'here are the things one should try to do' or "educate the organization on its potential consequences, and to give specific ideas for better ways to deal with the new and surprising" [2]. In that last passage, I argue the key words are *specific ideas* and *the new and surprising*. Yes, when building strategic futures exercises, it should allow for expansive thinking but provide a framing for detailed strategies and tasks defined within. The challenge is to strike a balance between having no limits and parameters that are too restrictive. The goal is to build something useful and resilient. This will be demonstrated in later sections of this textbook.

2.1 Why Strategic Planning Can Fail

Research cited by Harvard Business Review shows that a significant percentage, ranging from 60 to 90% of strategic plans fail to reach full implementation [3]. The reasons for this failure vary, but poor execution is consistently identified as a major contributing factor. While this assessment is often accurate, it does not provide the complete picture. The design of the strategy itself can also be a significant issue, even though acknowledging this may be challenging. They fail because they lack value or are not operationalized into action. They fail because the environment in which they were designed—the specific time and context—changed. More appropriately, the failure is in the capacity to meet the goals in a strategic plan. I use the word capacity intentionally as it can be expressed as a combination of two attributes within a workforce: capability and desire, or the more rhyming and memorable, skill and will. Some combination of the two attributes is needed to achieve anything, certainly something as expansive as an organization's long-term and overarching strategic plan.

Former Secretary of Defense, Donald Rumsfeld, was known for frequently sending out concise memos, referred to as "snowflakes," to his staff. One particular snowflake that garnered renewed attention is titled "Predicting the Future," dated April 12, 2001, just five months before the terrorist attacks that would significantly alter US foreign policy [4]. In this memo, Rumsfeld advised President George W. Bush to review a one-page caution prepared by Pentagon official Lin Wells for the 2001 Quadrennial Defense Review. Wells illustrated how the developments that shaped world affairs in each decade of the twentieth century did not align with what could have been anticipated at the beginning of each decade. He concluded by stating, "I'm not sure what 2010 will look like, but I'm certain that it will be vastly different from our expectations, and therefore, we should plan accordingly." This memo serves as a stark reminder of the unpredictability of the future and the importance of being prepared for unforeseen circumstances. It highlights the need for strategic planning that considers the ever-changing nature of global events. And here again, I return to the idea that a holistic approach, one that is not just plausible in its formulation, but also is presented in a compelling manner as to capture the attention of the whole of the organization, is obligatory. As strategic planners, we owe this, at the very least, to our senior leaders, decision makers and fellow employees.

In the following sections of this textbook, I offer a process to deliver a new 'product.' Storycasting is not simply about creating future scenarios; it is about presenting qualitative data and plausible futures in a more compelling way. This, however, is not assumed to be a traditional method of preparing information. In an organization where employees and leadership expect information presented in bulletized form, this may be a challenge. It might take some trial and error. And it might take some willingness to overcome challenges.

2.2 Challenge: Resistance or Apprehension

Strategic plans often involve a call for transformation, and resistance to change from within the organization can impede progress. Creating compelling narratives or futures scenarios can be a new concept in organizations. It should be expected that creating 'stories' is in direct opposition to the 'briefing.' Employees might resist new processes, technologies, or organizational structures, which would hinder the successful execution of the plan. It often sounds like *"That's not the way we do things here."*

Be alert for language that promotes stagnation from leadership and senior stakeholders as well. One phrase I've heard is *'We cannot make recommendations that our leaders won't support.'* If that idea is present, then I would suggest the leadership define what they can support before any new vision or strategy is explored. Where do senior leadership or decision makers stand in regard to change? Without the best information available, conservative views may prevail.

Let us assume that senior leadership holds the responsibility of crafting a strategy that creates and captures a specific goal and method. All too often those failures occur because their approach to strategy isn't holistic [5]. Some leaders tend to make different mistakes. Some underestimate how much new technologies or processes can increase value or productivity or efficiency. These leaders either ignore some components of what could be seen as the complete breadth of the trends—or critical uncertainties—or do not recognize the interdependencies among them. Refer back to the STEEPLE categories.

Again, there are multiple reasons why organizations fail to achieve strategic goals, but here are some that connect to the idea of Storycasting and making plausible futures into something more compelling. Authors of *Thinking About the Future*, Andy Hines and Peter

Bishop, state "Too many narratives were ending up on the shelves because the organization was unclear about how to use them" [2, p. 72]. It is not uncommon that objectives within a strategic plan are ambiguous or not well-defined and becomes challenging for the employees at all levels to align their efforts and measure progress effectively. Many are left asking "Why is this a priority?" or "What is the value behind this?" Successful execution of a strategic plan requires clear communication across all levels of an organization. If stakeholders are not involved in the meaning behind the goals and their roles in achieving them, it can lead to disengagement. Possibly, the best way to ensure the goals within the plan are understood is if participation in its development is not restricted.

2.3 Challenge: Lack of Explicitness to the Organization

There is an argument to be made that failing to meet strategic goals often occurs when it is not—or cannot be—operationalized because they lack specificity. When not operationalized, we see the common "document on a shelf" problem. All this time, energy (and money) has been essentially wasted when a plan isn't put into action [6] and it becomes another piece of 'wallpaper.'

Misaligned goals pose a significant challenge to achieving strategic success and serve as a clear indicator of a flawed strategy. A study conducted in 2020 revealed that only 51% of companies make an effort to establish goals aligned to their strategic plan, with only 6% consistently revisiting them [7]. It is crucial for the entire organization to be actively engaged in aligning goals, not just senior leaders. When departments and teams have conflicting objectives, for instance, it leads to disjointed strategy execution, inefficiencies, and ultimately, suboptimal performance. This lack of alignment perpetuates departments divisions working in the stereotypical silos rather than collaboratively. The study—as does others—contends that organizations with misaligned strategic objectives tend to experience weaker outcomes compared to their strategically aligned counterparts.

Like the need to track a history of a trend, new strategic plans must consider previous iterations. Any new strategy introduced must be considered within the context of previous plans. Its success or failure is influenced by the precedents set by past strategies as a way of creating longevity and broader vision. The perception of the strategy as temporary or permanent by frontline employees can significantly impact how the organization responds, regardless of executive directives. Leaders must carefully assess how the company's culture may affect the implementation of the strategy and address any internal barriers during the rollout process [3]. This involves not only the positioning, messaging, and packaging of the strategy but also the behaviors exhibited by leadership. By acknowledging past issues with previous initiatives and embodying key elements of the new strategy, such as prioritizing employee feedback, leaders can set a convincing foundation for successful implementation.

2.4 Challenge: Employee Disengagement

Employee engagement is a crucial factor in determining the success of a company's strategic initiatives. It serves as a vital link between the workforce and the overall business strategy. When employees are disengaged, it can be a clear indication of a failing strategy, often stemming from a lack of understanding about how their roles contribute to the organization's goals. As Ken Blanchard wrote, "Connect the dots between individual roles and the goals of the organization. When people see that connection, they get a lot of energy out of work" [3]. When employees feel that their work is insignificant, they may view their tasks as mere checkboxes on a list, lacking purpose and motivation.

It is important to maintain the level of engagement beyond the conclusion of a workshop or data collection initiative. Additionally, avoid oversimplifying the complexity and intricacies for the convenience of presenting information in a concise bullet-point format on a slide. Make strategic foresight (workshops—thinktanks—projects—working groups) "as immersive and interactive as possible" [2]. Empower employees to become true subject matter experts in the various aspects of the business or mission that they are dedicated to supporting. By fostering a culture that values and encourages continuous learning and development, employees will be equipped with the knowledge and skills necessary to excel in their roles and contribute meaningfully to the organization's success. This approach not only enhances employee engagement and satisfaction but also strengthens the overall capabilities and effectiveness of the team.

Lack of engagement can have a significant impact on efficiency. Gallup Poll showed that engaged employees can increase productivity by 17% and profitability by 21% [7]. Fostering a culture of employee engagement is not only beneficial for individual employees but also for the overall success of the organization. By ensuring that employees understand the importance of their contributions and feel connected to the company's strategic objectives, businesses can create a more motivated and productive workforce.

2.5 Challenge: Misunderstanding the Internal Culture

An organization's cultural context serves as a framework for employees to evaluate the viability of a new strategic plan. For instance, if we can all imagine how an organizational tendency to implement short-lived initiatives is often referred to as having 'flavor-of-the-month' strategies. These initiatives would be launched with great excitement, only to quickly lose relevance as a new one took their place. Sometimes those initiatives lack a deeper perspective. One that incorporates organizational-wide perspectives. It is not uncommon for an organization to create a goal or initiative to address a shortcoming, overlooking the impact the success or change would have elsewhere.

For instance, in 2013 the prominent parcel delivery company, UPS, introduced a new shipping initiative in anticipation of the holiday season. A relatively close horizon, but for

2.5 Challenge: Misunderstanding the Internal Culture

the context of this book, contextualize this as a future-based initiative as it was developed in anticipation or in preparation and planning was done with an imminent future in mind. To increase deliveries, they made significant investments in acquiring much-needed new aircraft and vehicles to enhance its delivery capabilities. However, the company encountered logistical challenges in training new personnel to load and unload the new aircraft and vehicles. It was too late to adjust. The delivery hubs that connected the aircraft and vehicles were not prepared for the increase in flow, creating choke points that nullified their intended benefits. In short, fixed one problem, creating another. The ambitious shipping initiative underscored the importance of a more comprehensive and holistic approach to strategic planning. It highlighted the need for effective training programs and contingency plans to ensure smooth operations during peak seasons—ideas that could have been reflected by scenario planning or broader inclusion in their strategic thinking. This is a real-world example of what can be seen as a myopic view of the future landscape as the company underestimated the surge in demand that ensued, leading to overwhelming challenges for its workforce and delivery teams [8]. If the output of a foresight effort results in goals that can be found in any other organization's or even an institution working in another industry or field, then the effort may not have been as specific to your organization as you'd hoped.

Assess your strategic plan. When chatgpt.com was asked, "What are typical goals in a strategic plan?" it produced the following within seconds. It found key phrases (examples? clichés? tropes?) from the mass of information on the Internet.

1. Financial Goals: These might include targets for revenue growth, profit margins, cost reduction, or increased shareholder value.
2. Market Goals: These could involve expanding market share, entering new markets, increasing brand awareness, or improving customer satisfaction and loyalty.
3. Product/Service Goals: Organizations often set goals related to developing new products or services, improving existing ones, or innovating to meet changing customer needs.
4. Operational Goals: These focus on enhancing efficiency and effectiveness in internal processes, such as supply chain management, production, distribution, or customer service.
5. Human Resources Goals: Goals in this area might involve attracting and retaining top talent, fostering employee development and engagement, or creating a diverse and inclusive workplace culture.
6. Sustainability Goals: Increasingly important, these goals pertain to environmental and social responsibility, such as reducing carbon footprint, promoting ethical sourcing, or supporting community initiatives.
7. Technology Goals: With rapid technological advancements, organizations often set goals related to digital transformation, cybersecurity, data analytics, or leveraging emerging technologies to gain a competitive edge.

8. Strategic Partnerships: Goals may include forming strategic alliances, collaborations, or partnerships with other organizations to access new markets, technologies, or resources.
9. Regulatory and Compliance Goals: Ensuring compliance with relevant laws and regulations is crucial, so goals related to legal compliance, risk management, and ethical conduct are common.
10. Long-Term Vision: Beyond short-term objectives, strategic plans often include aspirational goals aligned with the organization's long-term vision and purpose.

Using a highlighter, note words or ideas that are mirrored (even phrases word-for-word) in your organization's strategic plan. This ubiquitous language can apply to any organization or industry. It is uncompelling and lacks any evidence that self-reflection or an organization's particular mission or market needs have been examined. Or, that the information provided to senior leadership or decision makers was distilled or summarized so much that insights were lost. If an organization's strategic plan could be applied in any other industry, is it meaningful? If it uses broad language that can be interpreted differently across an organization, how can it guide behaviors, create measurable goals, or create focus for enterprise-wide efforts?

2.6 Opportunity in Story Casting: Everyone Is a Participant or Contributor

Consider strategic planning or futures efforts as a form of human-centered design. Not long ago, this concept was unfamiliar to many, but now it has become a fundamental requirement in various industries. The widespread adoption of human-centered design is signaling a significant evolution in our approach to problem-solving. As organizations delve deeper into this practice, some are witnessing a rapid advancement in its maturity. The argument behind human-centered design is that it makes it less likely to limit details, perspectives, and potential when a variety of collaborators are involved from the beginning, rather than discovering issues during testing at the end [2]. From the outset of strategic planning and futures work, incorporating a human-centric approach will enhance both the overall planning and anticipatory experience, but also the operationalizing of planning, goal setting, and mission outcomes.

Collaboration and commitment to co-create stem from a shared goal of uncovering fresh ideas and insights that may not have emerged otherwise. By adopting a user-centric perspective, organizations can develop solutions that address the root causes of problems, rather than merely treating their symptoms. Further, empathy for all the end users or implementers—which includes the senior leaders, employees, or customers—is a key component of human-centered design.

We can encourage active engagement by prompting the listener to use their imagination through thought-provoking questions such as "What occurs…" or "How do you react when…." [7]. Creating a compelling and engaging narrative can be done more easily by including original quotes and anecdotes from the participants. By incorporating these firsthand accounts into the story, readers are able to gain insight into the emotions, thoughts, and experiences of the participants who created the data. Overall, incorporating original quotes and anecdotes into a narrative can greatly enhance its impact and effectiveness by bringing it to life in a way that summary ideas—again, bullet points—simply cannot. The unconscious mind processes stories as explicit directives. This prompts the listener to visualize scenarios in order to respond effectively.

By engaging in a human-driven process—or rather, engaging more people into the process—you will be constructing something closer to an ethnography. With the goal of gaining a comprehensive understanding of the community as a whole or a specific issue affecting it [9]. This involves delving deeply into the lives of the population, obtaining insights from an insider's perspective (known as the emic perspective), grasping the significance attributed to the research topics, and establishing a cultural theory as the foundation of the research.

2.7 Opportunity in Storycasting: Storytelling as a Leadership Skill

Storytelling and futures scenarios have a long history. Nearly seven hundred years ago, Nostradamus penned his famous quatrains, which continue to captivate our imaginations. His popularity soared due to his ability to craft compelling yet enigmatic prose that reflected some grand narrative of humanity. Nostradamus foretold of uprisings, invasions of tyrants, ecological disasters, and the advancement of perilous weaponry. We know his name and we know his work not because his quatrains are accurate or can be remotely proven. We know Nostradamus as either a prophet or charlatan, but either way he was a masterful storyteller.

Storytelling is a valuable method for relaying statistical meaning in a professional setting because it allows complex data to be presented in a more engaging and understandable way. By incorporating storytelling techniques, such as using real-life examples or in this case anecdotes or plausible futures, dry statistics and bullet points can be contextualized and brought to life for the audience. This helps to not only capture their attention but also make the information more memorable and impactful. Additionally, storytelling allows for the human element to be infused into the data, making it easier for individuals to emotionally connect with the numbers and understand their significance. Ultimately, by utilizing storytelling as a tool for conveying statistical meaning, professionals can effectively communicate insights, trends, and key takeaways from data in a more compelling manner that resonates with their audience.

I would argue that online digital media also influences the way people digest information. Increasingly people consume information from online news articles and social media platforms—as brief forms of written or video delivery methods. Skipping any criticisms of this trend, I offer that it may shorten our attention spans, but also suggests we are increasingly gravitating toward narratives or stories as our favored delivery method of information. So why not lean into this trend and consider storytelling as a skill to be valued?

In *The Culture Code*, Daniel Coyle speaks to a simple question, "How can a handful of simple, forthright sentences make such a difference in a group's behavior?" [10]. Science has long informed us that a few isolated areas of our brain light up, translating words and images. Functional magnetic resonance imaging (fMRI) pinpoints specific areas of the brain responsible for translating words and images. These isolated regions, known collectively as language centers, play a crucial role in the processing of information related to speech and visual stimuli.

Coyle also pushes us to understand how narratives or stories can "guide group behavior" even though a story is seemingly intangible or ethereal [11]. Robert Rosenthal utilized a groundbreaking intelligence assessment tool known as the Harvard Test of Inflicted Acquisition to identify students with exceptional potential for intellectual development. He allowed teachers to select students they felt possessed the greatest potential of success. Then, a year later, he came back to discover the selected students achieved the teacher's perceived results; their test scores were indeed higher than the rest of the student population. However, the test was actually a deception, allowing Rosenthal to manipulate teachers (let us call them *the senior leaders*) into leading these selected students (let us call them *the workforce*) with increased warmth, providing them with more guidance, and offering enhanced feedback on their academic performance. This study sheds light on the power of expectations in influencing outcomes and underscores the importance of fostering a supportive and nurturing learning environment. I relay this story here because I think it shows how information or perception of something becomes more compelling or convincing when a narrative is provided. The teachers' behaviors were changed, Rosenthal argued, because he allowed them to create the narrative—or goals—they determined should be achieved.

Thomas Friedman tells us to value "the Great Explainers." These are the people who can understand the complexity of an issue they know much about but also explain it with simplicity [12]. For example, he highlights the importance of having individuals who are skilled in software distribution. However, it is crucial to have someone who can also effectively communicate with customers and articulate the benefits of the software. We want people at all levels of an organization to not only know their specialty front-and-back, but also people who can effectively This includes explaining how their efforts, in this case new software, will enhance current systems, potential risks, or any unintended consequences it might bring. This is storytelling at its core.

2.7 Opportunity in Storycasting: Storytelling as a Leadership Skill

Another influential voice in foresight and strategic planning, Amy Webb, advocates for storytelling as well. She provides different scenarios in a paragraph she calls "Sorting out real trends from red herrings" [13]. She demonstrates how alternate narratives create the probable, the plausible, and the possible. Webb encourages us to focus on "details, not just data" [14]. The utility of a short story that includes people and their behaviors and the practicality of application, not just the technology.

Humans are hard-wired to create meaning out of even partial information. We have an innate need to fill in the blanks, to structure information, and make sense of it. Ask yourself; *How often do I hear a rumor that's purpose is nothing more than assumptions? Or, said another way, is it just filling gaps of an incomplete story?* In the context of the workplace and strategic goals, if an employee is unaware of the *how* and *why* behind a goal, they are more inclined to create their own assumptions and assume other's intents behind the goals. There is supporting research behind this as well.

In a study conducted in 1944, two psychologists tasked thirty-four college students to watch a soundless short film depicting three different black shapes moving in and out of a rectangle [15]. Surprisingly, all but one student described the scene as a bully triangle chasing a little worried circle and a small innocent triangle. The students anthropomorphized the geometric shapes, attributing intentions, and emotions to them. The mesmerizing nature of the video made it difficult to interpret the bigger triangle, which only moved in one direction from one of its points, as an angry and intimidating figure.

This study highlights the innate human tendency to create narratives and stories, even from simple geometric shapes. The act of storytelling is deeply ingrained in human existence, as evidenced by the narratives of dreadful futures that have been published centuries apart. This study sheds light on the power of storytelling and the human mind's ability to find meaning and create stories from even the most basic stimuli.

Herman Kahn, a physicist working at the Rand Corporation, might be likened to a modern-day Nostradamus. During the 1950s, he was tasked with aiding military strategists in confronting unsettling scenarios that many were hesitant to consider. Questions such as, *what would happen if the Soviets were to launch a thermonuclear attack on New York City?* Or *how could the city be evacuated quickly and safely?* His approach involved crafting narratives—fictional stories based on the 'if this, then what' formula, designed to be read as reports from the future. However, Kahn encountered a dilemma. He did not want the military to dismiss his work as mere science fiction, nor did he want them to take it too seriously and mistake the narrative illustrations for factual predictions, as none of the stories presented definitive outcomes.

To address this issue, Kahn sought a new term to describe the work of his team. Collaborating with a humorist in Hollywood, they borrowed the term "scenario" from the film industry, which at the time referred to what we now know as a "screenplay". [16] The deeper neurological truth is that stories do not cloak reality but create it, "triggering cascaded of perception and motivation" [17]. When we encounter words or images, signals are sent to these specialized areas, triggering neural activity that allows us to interpret and understand what we see or hear. This scientific knowledge has numerous practical applications, from improving language learning techniques to developing more effective communication strategies in various professional fields.

> **Improved Understanding Through Storytelling and a Human-Centric Approach to Operational Decision Making.**
> Return back to the opening of this textbook, to my story about Haitian Migration. Use it as an analogy or metaphor. In that plane, the 'decision makers' were the two pilots. The three aircrew were 'department heads or mid-level leaders.' Collectively, we were making decisions about where and how we flew our sorties. We repeated the accepted practices from previous deployments and did not deviate from our expectations. We knew human migration patterns followed a north-northwest route along the island chain. We knew the data showed migration routes and where previous aircraft patrols found the boats and where surface ship interdictions occurred. We also had highly detailed weather information. All of the information we needed was in our pre-deployment briefing before we took to the air each day. What we lacked was any insight into human behavior. We failed to consider how people create their own story. Consider the following information and see what STEEPLE themes are now included in the narrative.
>
> It's the fall of 2004. The previous summer, hurricanes Ivan and Jeanne touched Haiti. First, Ivan caused flood damage across the country. Within months, Jeanne crossed western section of Haiti, killing 3,000 people, injuring thousands more and displacing over 300,000 from their homes. In any country storms and earthquakes remove opportunities for safety. Historically more so in Haiti.
>
> You are Phillipe Massard, the owner of a tattered but reliable wooden sailboat in Port-de-Paix, Haiti. With it, you earn a living ferrying everything from vegetables to charcoal to people between islands. Your boat is your livelihood. You maintain the hull and sails diligently. It is your most valuable possession, worth more than even your house. Today, you planned on taking twenty passengers on a two-day voyage north to Grand Turk Island. You are the only person with the ability or tools to navigate along your intended east-to-northeast heading.
>
> Word spreads of your trip, and forty people show up at the pier. All forty people pay you (relative to the yearly earning potential in Haiti) an exorbitant amount of money. They want you to transport them north in hopes of finding a seasonal job at one of the vacation resorts or in a local market. With the money they hope to earn, they can build a safer, more sustainable life. The boat is overloaded already, leaving little freeboard in calm seas. Though each person has their own narrative

2.7 Opportunity in Storycasting: Storytelling as a Leadership Skill

and individual reasons, all have literally gambled their lives on this trip to Grand Turk.

Early the second day, the weather turns. The waves get rougher and the wind changes direction. From years of experience, you know that at the very least these winds will extend your trip another day. At worst, the waves will soon fill your sluggish sailboat with water. You know that the US Coast Guard always has ships and aircraft patrolling the area. After two days, has a fear of drowning at sea led some passengers to want to be found by American ships or planes? In doing so, the ship's crew will take all of you onboard, provide food and medical care, and ensure everyone is repatriated back to Haiti. Your boat, if it's not already sinking, will be declared unseaworthy and intentionally sunk as a hazard to navigation.

Questions: What are your motives and threats as the boat owner? What are the motives and threats of your passengers? What will they do if a plane or aircraft spot you; wave for help or hide inside the cramped cabin? What can you do with your passengers? You could turn around and sail all the way back to Haiti and refund everyone their money. You could continue sailing and hope for the best.

Answer: You alter your course to the nearest island. Which in this case is the island of Inagua, a short sail directly east of your current position. When the boat is in waist deep water just off the beach, you will tell your passengers "Grand Turk is right there; just wade to shore," because you will never see these people again. That assumes that you arrive their safely and do not sink, losing all forty lives and your own.

Result: You either abandon your passengers at Inagua or sink at sea. Regardless, the US Coast Guard does not interrupt your trip, nor provide life-saving assistance to you and your passengers.

There were countless well-told stories of migrants being dropped off in just this manner. One with a particularly disastrous ending for the passengers. For unknown reasons, just as Phillipe Massard planned to do, one boat owner sent his passengers to wade ashore to—what he told them was—their desired destination. The sailboat was long gone when the disembarked passengers were discovered climbing a chain-link fence. Ironically and unfortunately for the passengers, he'd dropped them off on a well-manicured beach adjacent to the family housing section of the US Coast Guard base in Aguadilla Puerto Rico. Exactly where many aircraft used in migrant searches are based.

We knew that story, but it wasn't included in our assessment that day. Weather is only one of many factors that impact the never-ending cycles of human migration around the Caribbean. We didn't take our assessment of the situation down to *the person*. Once you consider the dimensions of human experiences in that small and dangerously overloaded boat you can begin to challenge your expectations. There is no assurance that considering all of the STEEPLE categories would change a particular decision on a particular day, but if it was part of our mission planning, we would have included more dimensions to our decisions.

References

1. Tetlock PE, Gardner D (2015) Superforecasting. Broadway Books, New York
2. Hines A, Bishop P (2015) Thinking about the future. In: Guidelines for strategic foresight, 2nd edn. Hinesight, Houston
3. Olson AB (2022, June 24) 4 common reasons strategies fail. Harvard Business Review. Retrieved 15 Mar 2024 from https://hbr.org/2022/06/4-common-reasons-strategies-fail
4. Hoehn A, Parasiliti A, Wyne A (2018, April 5) Can Washington successfully prepare for the future? Retrieved on 2 May 2024 from https://nationalinterest.org/feature/can-washington-successfully-prepare-the-future-25235?nopaging=1
5. Collis DJ (2021, July-August) What do so many strategies fail? Leaders focus on the parts rather than the whole. Retrieved 15 Apr 2024 from https://hbr.org/2021/07/why-do-so-many-strategies-fail
6. King M (2023, May 10) Why strategic plans fail. Envisio. Retrieved on 15 Mar 2024 from https://envisio.com/blog/why-strategic-plans-fail/
7. 6 signs of strategy failure. Quantive. Retrieved on 1 May 2024 from https://quantive.com/resources/articles/strategy-failure
8. Blanchard K, Blanchard S (2011, July 17) Do your people really know what you expect from them? Fast Company. Retrieved on 1 May 2024 from https://www.fastcompany.com/1767714/do-your-people-really-know-what-you-expect-them
9. Damon C (2024) 13 notorious examples of strategic planning failure. Achieveit. Retrieved on 1 May 2024 from https://www.achieveit.com/resources/blog/13-notorious-examples-of-strategic-planning-failure/
10. Gavin M, Oliver L (2024, April) Transforming public service: the human by design approach. Fedgovtoday.com Audio Podcast. Retrieved on 17 May 2024 from https://fedgovtoday.com/podcast/transforming-public-service-the-human-by-design-approach
11. Hadnagy C (2011) Social engineering. The art of human hacking. New York, Wiley
12. Hennick M, Hutter I, Bailey A (2011) Qualitative research methods. Sage, Los Angeles
13. Coyle D (2018) The culture code. The secrets of highly successful groups. Bantam Books, New York
14. Coyle D. pg 177
15. Friedman TL (2007) The world is flat. Picador, New York
16. Webb A (2016) The signals are talking. Why today's fringe is tomorrow's mainstream. New York, Hatchette Book Group
17. Webb, p 217
18. Webb, 219
19. Coyle, p 182

Making It Compelling 3

How do we turn the plausible into the compelling? I'm not completely sure yet, but I've been experimenting. I am convinced, however, that potential futures, with their plausible opportunities and threats, can be presented more convincingly than the basic spreadsheet or slide deck offers. Routinely, there is more than enough qualitative data from a workshop to create a realistic and compelling story akin to a Toffler's *simulated environment* or maybe a foresight biosphere (a term I'm playing with) where many critical uncertainties influence one another. The same scenario could be presented as a future news article, a simulated government or corporate position paper or stockholder report, or fictitious feature in an industry journal. Each of these formats creates different opportunities to present the plausible as compelling. Some formats would resonate more with government agencies, private industries, or consulting firms—depending on their relationship to the topic—so finding the right fit is equally important.

Senior leaders and decision makers often rely on hard data and evidence, but they also need to be inspired. Sometimes, all the charts and graphs in the world can't get people to pay attention. It cannot always *inspire action*. When we talk about the future, we shouldn't try to sound too sure of ourselves. Instead of saying we can predict what will happen, we should focus on the unique ideas and stories that foresight can give us. Let's use creativity to imagine what might come next.

As discussed earlier, a strategic plan serves as a crucial tool for achieving competitive advantage or mission success. It necessitates a comprehensive understanding of the organization's current position, goals, capabilities, as well as those of its competitors, customers' needs, and—depending on its position in the private or public sector—the overall industry or government undercurrents. However, developing a well-thought-out strategy is just the beginning. It is essential to effectively communicate and ensure understanding of the strategy to motivate action among those responsible for its implementation. Unfortunately, many strategy documents and presentations fall short in this aspect. Research indicates that only 28% of managers are able to identify three of their company's strategic priorities, let alone know what priorities and threats were considered when building them [1]. Stories can serve as a powerful tool to bridge the gap between strategy development and execution, intentions and outcomes, and strategists and implementers.

3.1 From Bullets to Believing

Take a moment to imagine a slide with a series of bulletized sentences. That cannot be hard, considering the image has been imprinted in your mind from the countless presentations and virtual training and every other time you have been fed information in its most abbreviated form. Actually, some of those bullets may not even be more than fragmented sentences. Bullet points are intended to highlight key points and assist readers in quickly scanning through large amounts of information. However, in practice, they can sometimes have the opposite effect. While initially used with good intentions to simplify and enhance readability, overuse of bullet points can make a document tedious to read and outdated in appearance. Since their rise to supremacy in high-level papers, bullet points have become a common feature elsewhere—even news reporting. Yet, their widespread use does not guarantee a modern or sleek look. In fact, when used inappropriately, bullet points can confuse readers rather than clarify information. One common pitfall is when authors rely on bullet points to present more complex ideas or a sequence in thought or rationale, which can lead to a lack of coherence and logical flow.

Even the accepted 'rules' of slide management—where most bullets make their home—limit the amount of information available. Many people accept that slides should have anywhere from five to seven bullets. This also dictates the maximum number of lines, or words on a slide. Or worse, you might be bound by the "Rule of Three." In an online article that advocates for this format, the author argues that having only three bullets allows for a clear and concise presentation of information, making it easier for the audience to digest and retain key points [2]. This is far too restrictive and summarizing for the complex information created in multiple plausible futures with a ten- or twenty-year horizon, isn't it?

Utilizing bullet points can be an effective strategy when presenting a complex argument or analysis. By breaking down your points into concise bullets, you can enhance clarity and comprehension for your audience. Each idea is presented sequentially, allowing the reader to digest the information in a structured manner. However, a bullet list alone does not constitute a compelling argument. Frequently, the efficiency of a set of bullets does not always yield the desired results. Instead, we fool ourselves into illusion of transparency [3] which can hinder the effectiveness of bullet points in conveying a persuasive argument. Brevity is not always better.

One of the most flagrant miscalculations in the history of bulletized information in a PowerPoint presentation was explained in the noteworthy article *Death by PowerPoint: the Slide that Killed Seven People*. I will distill the findings to this simple idea: A room full of senior leaders and decision makers at NASA agreed that the Space Shuttle Columbia was safe to return to earth's atmosphere even though the most significant slide clearly outlined that the piece of debris used in their test was roughly 600 times smaller than the size that punctured the wing during launch. They had all the information but did not have it presented in a way that told the full story. The information was right in front of them, and they thought it was telling them the damage was insignificant, and the shuttle would survive reentry. I encourage everyone who produces slideshows in their workplace—especially those with technical information—to read the article themselves.

Persuasion plays a pivotal role in all aspects of decision making and leadership. It is essential to convince others to see the potential risks or opportunities, to rally employees and colleagues behind a new strategic plan, or to secure partnerships in building cohesive measures of resilience in a yet-to-be realized future. Despite its undeniable importance, many struggle to effectively communicate and inspire others [4]. Oftentimes, they become entangled in the trappings of corporate or organizational jargon, again relying on summary presentations, or dry memos. In those formats, and the competition for leadership's attention to any particular topic, even meticulously researched and well-thought-out summaries can be easily met with skepticism, indifference, or outright rejection.

The power of storytelling lies in its ability to illicit reactions, evoke emotions, and inspire action. It is not just a marketing tactic, but a crucial skill for entrepreneurs, business owners, and leaders looking to stand out when competing for the attention of leaders [5]. Equally, this is a method to build trust and rapport with your workforce is crucial. To cultivate this connection with your audience, it is essential to incorporate storytelling into your plausible futures. By sharing stories that reflect personality, values, and authenticity, you can create a strong emotional bond with leaders and those who will operationalize the recommendations or mitigations that are developed. It is important to recognize that many decisions are driven by emotions, which are then rationalized with logic. By utilizing storytelling, you can tap into the reader's emotions, inspiring them to act and overcome any doubts or fears they may have.

3.2 Public Sector Efforts

While Storycasting has great potential in the private sector, governments and the public sector also need this form of communication. Storytelling has always played a crucial role in the government and military. There are historical references where it has served as a powerful tool for conveying information, shaping narratives, and influencing decision-making processes. By presenting information in the form of a narrative, intelligence professionals are able to capture the attention of decision makers, enhance their understanding of complex issues, and guide their decision-making processes. In this way, storytelling has become an indispensable tool for intelligence agencies in effectively communicating critical information and shaping the perceptions and beliefs of key stakeholders.

3.2.1 Cartoons for the Greatest Generation

During World War II, graphic images were utilized as a powerful tool to educate and train soldiers on various aspects of warfare. One common use of graphic images was in the form of military manuals and training materials. These visuals often depicted detailed illustrations of tactics, weapons, and equipment, providing soldiers with a clear and comprehensive understanding of battlefield strategies. By presenting information in a visually stimulating manner, soldiers were able to absorb and retain knowledge more effectively, facilitating their readiness for combat. Civilians too were provided information through graphic design. Blackout reminders, information about how and where to seek shelter, and even patriotic encouragement messages were widely distributed through visual imaging on mass-produced posters and billboards. The power of a simple image was enough to relay subtle reminders and easy-to-understand mini-stories.

Graphic images were also used to document and convey the harsh realities of war to soldiers as a form of psychological preparation. Photographs and drawings depicting scenes of destruction, injury, and death were shown to soldiers to convey the brutal consequences of warfare and instill a sense of urgency and seriousness in their duties. By exposing soldiers to these graphic images, military leaders aimed to mentally prepare them for the challenges and horrors they may face on the battlefield, ultimately enhancing their resilience and adaptability in combat situations.

During World War II, the allied nations found themselves embroiled in conflicts in regions where they lacked knowledge of the economy, climate, and topography, as well as the attitudes and preoccupations of the local populations they aimed to liberate or ally with. This lack of understanding posed significant challenges for the Allies as they navigated unfamiliar territories and attempted to build relationships with the people they sought to support [6]. Historians, classicists, linguists, and philosophers all found their niche in intelligence and played significant roles in the events of World War II and every subsequent war. This is not limited to conflict; government and military entities continue to leverage storytelling.

3.2.2 Project Evergreen

The United States Coast Guard has historically been forced to prioritize short-term objectives due to the nature of its constant operational posture. With eleven statutorily mandated

3.2 Public Sector Efforts

missions, including fisheries protection and port security, the Coast Guard is frequently called upon to respond to emergencies such as, famously, Hurricane Katrina and the Deepwater Horizon oil spill. This constant demand for readiness underscores the organization's commitment to immediate action and operational efficiency.

Foresight practitioners within the US government frequently cite the Coast Guard's Project Evergreen as the benchmark for cyclical scenario planning exercises, even called a "gold standard" among federal agencies due to its longstanding operation and proven ability to connect future foresight with preparedness of actions [7]. The success of Project Evergreen has inspired other organizations, including the Federal Emergency Management Agency, to model their own efforts after its approach.

Launched in 2003, Project Evergreen followed its predecessor, Project Long View. This initiative came at a critical time for the Coast Guard, as the organization was facing significant organizational stress. The Homeland Security Act of 2002 had transferred the Coast Guard from the Department of Transportation to the newly established Department of Homeland Security. This transition resulted in a substantial increase in the Coast Guard's budget and a significant shift in the balance and scope of its mission. One goal of Project Evergreen, which is still very active within the service, is to improve the Coast Guard's ability to adapt to "change and surprise" and "to immunize the organization against a black swan," as a former senior leader explained [7]. The Coast Guard's experience serves as a compelling example of an organization navigating future uncertainty while continuing to operate in the present. This period of transition required the Coast Guard to adapt to new challenges and reevaluate its strategic priorities. Part of this ongoing effort, which leverages a scenario-based planning model, included the development of multi-page descriptions of the most compelling plausible future worlds. Two early examples of this effort were created well over a decade ago.

One of the first scenarios, titled *Code Quebec*, summarized a plausible world that, while never promising to be predictive, did provide some hauntingly recognizable themes. In *Code Quebec*, the first epidemic, "SARS 2," hit the United States in the mid-2000s, striking western port cities. Tens of thousands died in the worst epidemic since the flu of 1918. Global distrust crept into the issue, and political influences negatively impacted measures to halt the spread of disease. Subsequent strains of multi-drug-resistant tuberculosis (MDRTB) spread to the general population, and previous overuse of antibiotics guaranteed that its worst impact. American xenophobia, originally directed at foreign nations, now turned against fellow citizens. Towns "battened down the hatches," and strangers became unwelcome, while local and neighborhood solidarity also increased. "Living in the bubble" allowed a sense of safety.

In that same effort, Project Evergreen created *Forever War*. In this plausible future, a sense of prophecy appeared that even its authors would find surprising. In that scenario, the United States is strained due to constant and multiple global military deployments. Our economy is stretched thin under staggering debt and skyrocketing unemployment. Some populations are left feeling economically vulnerable in light of these circumstances. Many families rely on dual incomes and reside in multi-generational homes, yet social cohesion is strained. The political landscape is characterized by inter-generational conflicts and a multitude of adversarial political factions. The landscape is marked by hostility, confrontation, and an unwillingness to compromise. Single-issue politics and the vilification of opponents have become commonplace. It is evident that society is facing significant challenges, both economically and politically. The need for unity, cooperation, and a return to civil discourse is increasingly lost.

The full descriptions of both futures can be found online at:

https://www.uscg.mil/portals/0/Strategy/Report%20Evergreen%20I.pdf

3.2.3 Force Design 2030

In light of geopolitical changes, the US Marine Corps recognized strategic shifts are imperative. Senior leaders recognized the era following the Cold War had come to an end, and the international order—once upheld by the United States and its allies—is under threat from new centers of power, rogue nations, and non-state actors. While the United States continues to prioritize stability, peace, and prosperity on a global scale, the Marine Corps' methods employed to achieve these goals had to evolve.

The Marine Corps was confronted with the task of developing a modern fighting force, embracing experimentation, and adapting its organizational structure to keep pace with a changing strategic landscape. To accomplish this, a "maneuverist approach must be adopted at the institutional level" [8]. The recent conflict between Russia and Ukraine serves as a clear example of the changing nature of warfare.

The response—or futures-centric effort—is called Force Design 2030 (FD2030) and has provided a vision for the future, challenging the mindset of leaders at all levels, from senior officials to the rank and file of the Fleet Marine Force. This initiative outlined a comprehensive plan for modernizing the Marine Corps, fostering a sense of ownership, and driving action throughout the entire service. FD2030 provided Marine Corps leaders with a strategic framework to "outpace adversaries through rapid adaptation and innovation." However, FD2030 also acknowledged that responding to a crisis today and effectiveness on future battlefields necessitated continuous iteration and testing of scenarios they built. It could not be an effort with a beginning and an end.

The service is currently focusing on both the tactical and operational levels in the littorals (shoreline operational areas), with the goal of supporting the naval force and competing in contested maritime spaces as outlined in FD2030. The Marine littoral regiment serves as a testing ground to validate new and evolving scenarios in preparation for ongoing threats. Essentially, they built storytelling and realistic futures scenarios into their strategic planning.

3.3 Why Threatcasting?

Strategic planning and foresight work is not a one-size-fits-all endeavor. Threatcasting, as a methodology, looks ten years out into the future. Based on interdisciplinary inputs, the methodology allows participants to model a ranch of potential futures—sometimes up to thirty vignettes in a single workshop—and then examines how to disrupt, mitigate, and recover from the identified threats. Like other models, Threatcasting also begins with a research question [9]. A more academically rigorous process than a simple tabletop exercise, Threatcasting begins before participants enter the room. The process of defining the 'thesis question' with possible multiple sub-questions begins weeks before the multiday event begins. Further, rather than focus on two or three critical uncertainties, Threatcasting allows contributors, working in cohorts, to bring their subject matter expertise from multiple perspectives and apply them to multiple scenarios of their own design. In this way, they allow any or all STEEPLE themes to be mixed into any of the scenarios. When asked, here are some of the ways I usually describe Threatcasting:

> It is one of a handful of effective methodologies that systematically examines trends and then encourages participants to extrapolate those trends forward, usually using a 'look ten years in the future' context. Human-centric, it is the only model that begins with a specific character experiencing the 'threat.'
> Not a solitary endeavor, but communal. It empowers subject matter experts (SMEs), organized in cohort to collaborate from multiple domains. Through structured activities, and review of prepared presentations by academics and other SMEs, they are free to hypothesize plausible threats and new developments from their own perspectives.
> Its consistency and repeatability allow for longitudinal studies of findings across many workshops.
> The model does not simply ask participants to 'describe the threat' but also to 'describe the steps that lead to that future' and the likely ways to mitigate or interrupt it.
> The post-workshop analysis does not re-interpret or overly summarize findings but rather represents the original data and provides a synthesis back to the stakeholder's needs.

Threatcasting provides a level of specificity because its developers believed that traditional tools of foresight are necessary but not sufficient for the twenty-first century [10]. Threatcasting is a methodology that looks 10 years out into the future. Based on interdisciplinary inputs, it models a range of possible potential futures. Then participants backcast and provide clues to disrupt, mitigate, and recover from that threat.

This has been mentioned repeatedly; knowing a future state at a broader scale, say the industry or national level, is done very well through STEEPLE and scenario-based planning (SBP). It is a solid world-building technique and is easy to learn and apply, and it is highly repeatable. It can show senior stakeholders equally broad implications.

Consider grabbing the attention of the employee, midlevel manager, customer, or peer. That can sometimes lead to the challenges discussed earlier when strategic plans become too distant or lofty to engage the whole of an organization's workforce. World-building is effective at a large scale, but can leave individuals at any level of an organization wondering "Yes, but what is my role in that world?" or "How will that future impact me, specifically?" As strategic planners and foresight professional we can deliver something more, well, personal.

The power of personal stories lies in their ability to emotional responses. We all experience this when we enjoy a good book, television show, or movie. Even in news stories and reporting of an event a personal element can help capture our attention. In *Risk: The Science and Politics of Fear*, the author explains how using the power of personal stories is the root of most news reporting. "Introduce a person whose story is moving, connect that story to the larger subject at hand, discuss the subject with statistics and analysis, and close by returning to the person with the moving story" [11]. Personal narratives offer a human element that serves to resonate with viewers or readers, drawing them into the story on a deeper level. By showcasing real-life experiences and perspectives, these stories become relatable and engaging, holding the potential to leave a lasting impact on the audience. Any well-structured and methodological future foresight model or workshop can provide a world where personal perspective or narrative can theoretically exist. In Threatcasting, however, *the person* and the people around them are created at the very inception of that future world, not as an afterthought.

> ...because the future is designed by everyone, you cannot design a place without everyone's voice included. [The Threatcasting method] is kind of like an empathy hack. It's a way to sit in the place of a person imagining them experiencing something horrific and then you, working really hard as a participant, to walk it back to make sure it never happens.
>
> ...sometimes we can get veering off on the seduction of technology or whatever somatic thing we're looking at. But at the core, the reason we're doing it is for the human beings, and so built into the methodology is the link right on back to human beings.
>
> —Cyndi Coon, talking about *Threatcasting*.

When presenting a theoretical world to your leaders and workforce, the dimension of inhabitedness adds a layer of complexity and intrigue that attracts reader. This not only makes the theoretical world more dynamic but also provides storytelling possibilities that are more relatable to the reader. Even delving into the intricacies of cultures, histories, and relationships within this populated world, one can gain a deeper understanding of the human behaviors that create the future where threats exist, but also how they will create and perform the recovery from, and resilience to, those threats.

References

1. Reeves M, van Straten R, Nolan T, Michael M (2023, February 23) Your strategy needs a story. Harvard Business Review. Retrieved online on 10 May 2024 from https://hbr.org/2023/02/your-strategy-needs-a-story
2. May T (2018, October 2) Three reasons for three bullet points. CIO. Retrieved on 15 May 2024 from https://www.cio.com/article/222357/three-reasons-for-three-bullet-points.html
3. Funnel J (2016, May 21) Why bullets won't make your case. Emphasis. Retrieved on 3 Apr 2024 from https://www.writing-skills.com/bullets-wont-make-case
4. Fryer B (2003, June) Storytelling that moves people. Harvard Business Review. Retrieved on 12 Apr 2024 from https://hbr.org/2003/06/storytelling-that-moves-people
5. Geordiadis C (2023, June 8) The power of storytelling for your business. In: Unleashing your inner storyteller. Forbes. Accessed on 15 Apr 2024 from https://www.forbes.com/sites/theyec/2023/06/08/the-power-of-storytelling-for-your-business-unleashing-your-inner-storyteller/?sh=38b7e5e7fe09
6. Pettiggree A (2023) The book at war. How reading shaped conflict and conflict shaped reading. New York, Hatchette Book Group
7. Strategic foresight in practice: the case of the U.S. Coast Guard. New America. Retrieved on 22 Feb 2024 from https://www.newamerica.org/future-security/reports/strategic-foresight-in-us-agencies/strategic-foresight-in-practice-the-case-of-the-us-coast-guard/
8. Ellison KB (2023, April) Marine corps adaptation: the future is now. In: Proceedings. US Naval Institute, vol 149, no 4. Retrieved on 3 May 2024 from https://www.usni.org/magazines/proceedings/2023/april/marine-corps-adaptation-future-now
9. Johnson BD, Vanatta N, Coon C (2021) Threatcasting. In: Synthesis lectures on threatcasting. Morgan and Claypool, p 15
10. Lindsey G (2024, April 18) From bullets to belief: the power of storytelling through Sci-Fi prototypes. In: Connexions24 conference at UT Austin. https://www.youtube.com/watch?v=akpQRCaKLjg&list=PLHeilMXzC17fsOU50t8D8J5pul2JUrVN7&index=13
11. Gardener D (2009) Risk. In: The science of politics and fear. Virgin Books, London, p 108

Threatcasting to Storycasting—As Shown by Example

4

The Threatcasting process produces ample qualitative data. Primarily, a comprehensive academic report is produced after the analysis of the data is complete, themes are developed, and deeper implications and recovery from the threat are proposed. Immediately after the Threatcasting event participants often retain a copy of the workbooks—digital or paper—used in a workshop. They could or even should, if asked, present highlights or general themes to their leadership. Also, people who read the summary documents from a Threatcasting effort should present the relevant findings to decision makers in their organization, emphasizing the potential implications. What I envision is a better way to present this information to leadership and decision makers. And in turn, a better way for leadership to understand what decisions can be made about those threats and mitigations. I contend that decision makers have specific needs that can be better addressed.

- They need know if their company's position needs to change if the seemingly insignificant trend becomes the main driver of their industry.
- They can have a deeper understanding that adding more aircraft and trucks will create congestion in connecting hubs.
- They should see themselves in the future, understanding the risks of export agreements with one of the nation's trade allies if they join BRICS in 10 years.
- They should know if it is safe enough to bring Columbia home or if another shuttle should be sent up to rescue the astronauts.

The upcoming sections of this book will assist in transforming a plausible output from a Threatcasting workshop—a future scenario—into various formats that convey the data in a more compelling manner. The process of Storycasting follows after the completion

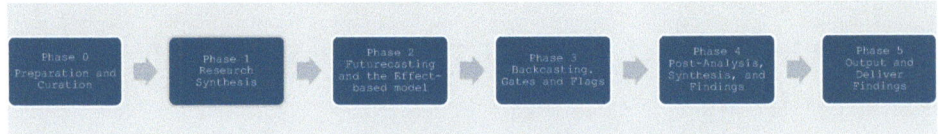

Fig. 4.1 A high-level overview of the Threatcasting process as described by the author

of the Threatcasting methodology outlined in the source document of the same name, *Threatcasting*, authored by the methodology's creators, Brian David Johnson, Natalie Vanatta, and Cyndi Coon. Their book delves into more detailed information regarding the development of the methodology, the different types of Threatcasting workshops, and the academic rigor associated with the method. For this section of the book, I will only provide a high-level summary of the Threatcasting steps and mirror them for their practical application in Storycasting. At a high level, and for the purposes outlined here, Threatcasting follows the below initial phases.

Phase 0: Preparation and Curation. Defining the topic and thesis.

Phase 1: Research Synthesis. Creation of the prompts—or questions—participants will use to develop their future scenarios, creating participant workbook, and preparation for the workshop.

Phase 2: Futurecasting and the Using the Effect-Based Model (EBM). Conducting the Threatcasting workshop and capturing the participant scenarios as they complete their workbook and answer the prompts.

Phase 3: Backcasting. Gates and Flags. Creating information that leads to recovery or resilience.

Phase 4: Post-Analysis and Synthesizing the Findings. An analysis team uncovers themes, novelty in the future scenarios and prepares summary documentation.

Phase 5: Output. Presenting of the final synthesis and findings.

Again, to explain the idea behind Storycasting, I will mirror the first three phases of the Threatcasting methodology. See Fig. 4.1. I will present a project as it would be created in Phase 0: Preparation and Curation. Then, as outlined in Phase 1: Research Synthesis, a set of research questions for the project and the workshop participant prompts will be presented. Then, following Phase 2: Futurecasting, where the actual workshop takes place, I will present a model or simulated output from a Threatcasting workshop. For Storycasting, we can include simulated findings that created by the participants in Phase 3: Backcasting.

At this point the Threatcasting methodology continues into other post-event activities such as analysis for high-level themes and takeaways. For the Storycasting model, however, analysis is not needed. Instead, we will diverge from the Threatcasting path and take the data collected and use it to experiment with storytelling or, more accurately, create

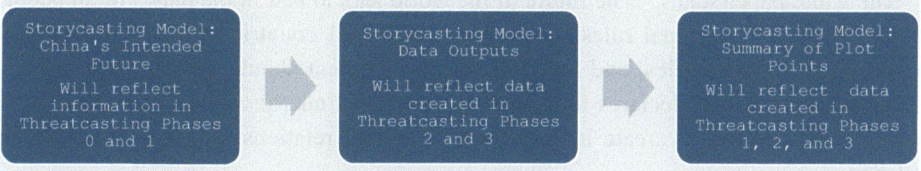

Fig. 4.2 A high-level view of the Storycasting process as described by the author

a story from the original data. We will use the raw data and walk through the simple process of developing it into short story using a template commonly referred to as the Three-Act Play. See Fig. 4.2. There will also be a mockup of a newspaper front page with multiple articles related to the story, a journal cover reflecting an industrial view of the event, and an after-action report from a law enforcement organization.

4.1 Storycasting Sample Exercise: China's Intended Future

In Threatcasting, the process begins with Phase 0 [1]. Preparation and curation comprise stakeholders determining the topic or the critical uncertainty they wish to explore. For this textbook and this theoretical exercise, I've selected a topic for our stakeholders, who might represent a specific organization that works in the domains of international relations, global development, or transnational infrastructure [2]. They could be policy experts or regulators or even investors. For their project—consider it akin to an academic research topic—the future scenarios and the Threatcasting workshop will focus on a specific document and a single, significant idea found within.

They—our stakeholders—have taken interest in China's economic expansion and want to explore a future, based on a Threatcasting ten-year horizon, how China's global development goals might be achieved, the potential impacts, and plausible global reactions to China. The source document used to stimulate or provide a framework for this project is a white paper published by China's State Council Information Office on December 4, 2021. This public document can be found online at many locations, including the website operated by The State Council of The People's Republic of China [3]. It has since been reprinted, highly reported-on, and scrutinized by global news outlets and governments around the world. It announces to the world, along with a clarification of Chinese Democracy, how all democracies should be characterized by policies that prioritize the needs of people, harness people's potential, and guarantee that people reap the rewards of growth. The white paper communicates that China is prepared to share in global political advancement through collaboration and mutual understanding. This rationale applies not only to their citizens as the Chinese government provides these needs and rewards, but globally and to the whole of humanity.

The white paper states, "The future of the world should rest in the hands of all peoples of the world. International rules should be made by all countries, global affairs should be governed by all parties, and the fruits of development should be shared by all" [3]. China's State Council declares they have and will continue, proactively cultivate global partnerships, aiming to create a framework of global relations that is both stable and balanced.

The stakeholders of this simulated Threatcasting effort focus on the language of the white paper as an intentional message from China that it has a plan to expand its development and economic expansion and challenge the global status quo. One key statement is highlighted by stakeholders that affirms, "Powerful countries should behave as befits their status, make the future of humanity their priority, and shoulder greater responsibility for world peace and development, rather than wielding their power in pursuit of supremacy or hegemony" [3]. With that focus, the Threatcasting project begins to research trends and other signals that will inform the upcoming workshop.

Certainly, China's white paper would be no surprise to the stakeholders and subject matter experts. During Phase 0: Preparation and Curation, efforts are made to research and incorporate relevant and related information into the project. Preparation includes some form of literature review and scoping of the issues related to the topic.

The preparation and curation phase included understanding current realities:

1. China is a permanent member of the UN Security Council and will join the Economic and Social Council in 2025 [4].
2. The African continent is vast and has the capacity to accommodate a large population, but the question remains: Can this growing population and developing nations achieve prosperity? What are the implications when 1.3 billion people are not actively engaged in the globalized economy? [5].
3. Brazil, Russia, India, China, South Africa (BRICS) nations continually seek new member nations and view global development as an opportunity for expansion [6].
4. The United Nations Millennium Development Goals (MDGs) and Sustainable Development Goals (SDGs) have been falling behind their envisioned benchmarks [7].

Using the above information as benchmarking for the topic (above is again, simply for demonstration purposes and a real workshop would involve more inputs) Phase 1: Research Synthesis requires the creation of the prompts—or questions—participants will use to develop their future scenarios, the creation of the participant workbook, and other preparations for the workshop [8]. This is not unlike the idea of identifying critical uncertainties as discussed earlier in scenario-based planning. For this simulated project, Fig. 4.3 provides the pre-workbook and the responses from the stakeholders and planners.

What is the topic (driver) of the Threatcasting Project (event, workshop) and what is the Thesis Question(s)?	Published by China's State Council Information Office in 2021, *China: Democracy That Works* outlines not only their model of democracy, but also their development goals for the globe and all of humanity. China's expansion in Africa and drive as a founding member of the growing BRICS coalition of nations is apparent. China intends to *"build a global community of shared future and presses for a new model of international relations based on mutual respect, fairness and justice, and win-win cooperation."* And also, their strategy *"promotes mutually beneficial exchanges and cooperation."* China contends *"The future of the world should rest in the hands of all peoples of the world. International rules should be made by all countries… …and the fruits of development should be shared by all."* Thesis Question(s): 1. How might China further their global development goals in the next ten years; turning their aspirations into actions? 2. In what ways can China share the 'fruits of development' with other - developing - nations and who are they? 3. Who (what nations or organizations) would support China in their goals?
Who is attending the Threatcasting Event (workshop, offsite)	Subject matter experts (or people who work in the domains of) in international relations, global development, transnational infrastructure. Regulators and policy experts. People who work in those domains as leaders, researchers, advisors, and those that would execute recovery or resilience to future threats.
When this final Threatcasting Report is complete, who's attention do you want to gain with its findings?	Decision makers in the economic sector, decision makers in large-scale infrastructure industry, people representing economic and development interests in the United States and Europe and possibly the IMF and/or World Bank. Fiction writers and screenplay writers. The report will be made public and will include no classified or otherwise sensitive content not suitable for public consumption.

Fig. 4.3 Scoping prompts the replies from the stakeholders and planners

4.2 Storycasting Model: Participant Output

Ideally, in a Large Group Threatcasting Workshop three dozen or so people would be asked to participate in the multi-day workshop. However, there are other saleable options such as Small Group workshops, Rapid, and Individual deliveries [9]. For this, we will assume a Large Group Threatcasting Workshop was held where participants were introduced to the project, the sequence of events over the next days, and given an opportunity to hear the perspectives of other SMEs who are asked to contribute their perspectives on the related trends. For the above topic SMEs might include, for instance, a retired member of the State Department or a senior leader from a large industrial corporation, a representative from an NGO or aid organization that does overseas business, or academics from any number of related disciplines related to the topic.

Threatcasting utilizes **effect-based modeling**. Effect-based modeling is like playing with blocks to see how they fit together and make a big tower. Instead of just looking at each block by itself, we look at how they all work together to create a big picture. For Threatcasting, it helps participants understand—and include in their explanations—how different events can cause changes or effects in a larger system of people or organizations. During Phase 2 workshop participants are provided a number of prompts to 'steer' their imagination and the 'blocks' they want to incorporate in each of their plausible future scenarios [10].

Three key pieces of information are needed for each scenario [11]. They include:

A person that the scenario revolves around.
A place where they exist or live.
The experience: problem or threat.

A Large Group Threatcasting workshop, sometimes referred to as a 'Big Tent,' has many participants, arranged in **cohorts**, that repeat the scenario creation process up to three times in two days. The developers of the methodology have found that Large Group Threatcasting workshops lend themselves to complex and multifaceted issues [12] and create many diverse and plausible futures to analyze. Think about it this way; Broad Trend: Large Group. Specific Trend: Small Group.

> It should be noted that effective and intentional facilitation during a Threatcasting workshop is important as groups can sometimes drift 'off task' from time to time, taking phone calls, doing some light professional networking, or even taking their conversations off topic.

Recalling that a scenario-based planning (SBP) efforts will normally produce four alternate futures with two intersecting themes or critical uncertainties (eight futures if three intersect), the Large Group Threatcasting workshops normally produce roughly three futures per cohort, using a comparable number of participants and workshop hours.

Following the same phases, but in a more focused scale, Small Group Threatcasting Workshops can operate with five to twelve participants [13]. An output from a group of participants work together to create a single complex scenario or repeat the process a few more times depending on how much time is available. Lastly, Individual Threatcasting, as the name suggests, runs a single person through the methodology, typically on a concentrated theme and focused effort [14].

Regardless of the number of groups or the size of each group, the data, or responses they provide typically appear as it does in Fig. 4.4. It should be acknowledged, that while the data provided for the Storycasting methodology in the subsequent pages was created by a single person—me, the author of this book—it too followed the prescribed key benchmarks needed to simulate a sample output from a "Big Tent" workshop.

Before moving on, take a few moments to read through all of the prompting questions on the left of the chart and how much detail can be provided by participants on the right of the chart. Responses normally vary in depth and detail; however, all data provided in all scenarios are included in the post-workshop analysis and final summaries. While not all Threatcasting cohorts produce data this comprehensive, the scenarios with the most robust information, generally speaking, tend to be included as examples in the publication(s) and summaries produced.

4.2 Storycasting Model: Participant Output

Part One: Who is your Person?	Participant Responses
Who is your person, what is their name, and what do they look like? How old are they?	• William Kittle. He's a 30+ year old African American. Tall and out of shape. Since his divorce (short marriage - no kids) not much of a personal life outside of his work. • William is a writer who quit his job teaching international relations at a midwestern state university to write full-time. He's been published in *The Atlantic, Wired* and others.
Who are their friends and what is their broader community?	• His colleague Kirsten. She used to teach Economics at the same university. Now she's working with European Financial and Economic Crime Centre (EFECC, a subset of Europol) from the US Dept of Treasury. Supervisor at DoT sent her overseas as a liaison – but really to get her out of his hair. She was sent on this detail "With a warning label." She is fluent in multiple languages. • His publishing agent, Andrea. She promotes/supports William's work. • Other people in William's community are other writers like him; academics, hackers, fixers, publishing professionals – and SMEs he interviews for his writing projects.
Where to they live? What is their occupation?	• William lives a vagabond life but currently living in the UK with a work visa through his UK-based publisher/agent. • William is currently working on a series of articles on European Infrastructure projects (dams, bridges, tunnels, buildings) and the major construction/development contracts in Asia and Africa.
What is going on in their world? What does a day in their life look like?	• William builds his own daily/weekly/monthly schedule but has to interview people in various industries. Think: Robert Young Pelton meets Tom Woodward, but not as charismatic. • Until he gets something published, he's not making any money, though he may get some up-front funding from publishers if they accept his book proposal. • He is beholden to his agent who promotes his work. • If EFECC does not take the novel threat seriously, he would be compelled to write an article about how they were incapable/unwilling to investigate.
What is the threat to their way of life?	• Because the laws/norms/applications of AI is still being developed, understanding how it could be a threat is complex. • A threat to the status quo: China, a key member of BRICS, is seeking to develop the whole of the world 'equally and fairly' – the whole of humanity, not just the 'first world.' IMF, NATO, World Bank, EU and all the G7-through-G20s may not believe/trust/support China's intentions. • After publishing a few articles about what he's learned, Kittle dies under mysterious circumstances. A threat to journalists: 2023 was deadly for journalists and the lack of trust in journalism/news as a whole is on the rise. If they are to continue to be a part of the news/information (free press, unfettered journalism) and relied upon to find/report what's going on behind the scenes in geopolitics, industrial development, global partnerships) will they become targets? Will the job of a journalist go away? Will foreign journalists be barred from certain countries? • Investigative and Regulatory Bodies: As older generations of senior leaders retire, will the traditional model of 'workers only work as directed and only leaders make decisions' change? If a junior financial investigator is not empowered to pursue a novel threat (Kirsten), will they leave that industry and move elsewhere? (like the white-hat hacker becoming a black-hat hacker).
How do they become involved in the scenario?	• William is doing the leg work for a larger piece of investigative journalism about new EU/China and EU/Africa infrastructure projects. He is at an interview with an industrial company when he "accidentally" takes a stack of papers off the floor. This includes an internal memo that suggests there is an AI-powered imaging program capable of hiding technical information in other digital documents – online journals, public-facing websites, e-books, etc. • In the following weeks, William learns that they'll use AI to layer the technical data – the designs and diagrams and specs – in other digitally-created images. Then anyone who knows where to look for them can replicate them. Otherwise, they will be 'hidden' in images.
Who else is involved?	• An unknown group of hackers. • Unknown industrial leaders from China, South Africa, and Brazil. • An unknown group of 'supporters' from the UN.

Fig. 4.4 Participant prompts and their responses to initial questions

More than just generalized ideas, participants or practitioners of the model are "required to think about the threat from multiple angles…" which enable them to build "a broader range of gurus while at the same time capturing a larger more detailed dataset" in the following phases [15]. Allowing participants to include whatever information needed to explain their plausible future, and the people that inhabit it, can serve as powerful tools in the unconscious mind's processing of information. These details act as direct instructions, prompting the participant to engage their imagination. For instance, facilitators may prompt participants by posing questions such as "What happens…" or "How do [the characters] feel when…", the participants are compelled to envision a scenario in order to respond. [16] This technique forces the participants to tap into their creativity and think beyond the surface level, ultimately enhancing their understanding and retention of the information being conveyed. More succinctly, think "Situation, Behavior, Impact" [17]. This is a part of storytelling, and a skill described in earlier chapters of this textbook. Even in the concise template used in the workshops, participants are encouraged to describe the situation, the observed behavior, and the perceived impact. This information would typically appear as seen in Fig. 4.5. Again, take a few moments to read through the prepared prompts on the left and the participant's responses on the right.

As you look through Figs. 4.4 and 4.5, you can already see the beginnings of a story. In its original form, the qualitative data begins to take shape and create a scenario complete with actors, actions, reactions, and challenges. Not all participants—even those working in cohorts—create equally robust details; however, the Threatcasting model provides enough prompts, inputs, and context for participants.

Part Two: Experience Questions	Participant Responses
When the person first encounters the threat, what will they see? What will the scene feel like? What will they not see or understand until later?	• William surreptitiously (and not exactly honestly) gets ahold of information from a German construction company, that they 1) knew their industrial design databases were hacked, and 2) China was going to back out of a multi-billion-dollar construction deal. Both of these pieces of information - the company fears- will ruin the company's future and will make them responsible for weakening future EU-centric infrastructure deals and East/West political impacts. • After working on the story some more, William presents what he's learned to his colleague, Kirsten. • Kirsten believes there is credibility to what William shares, however when Kirsten presents her initial findings to Senior Leadership at EFECC, their reactions reflect skepticism, archaic organizational structures, and unwillingness to risk resources investigating a novel crime that has not yet been committed.
What are the broader implications of a threat like this? What might a ripple effect look like?	• IMF and the World Bank may find a "Rising China" is inevitable but cannot politically support their goals. • As the UN is struggling to achieve its Millennium Development Goals, it finds itself an ally to BRICS nations (current and pending members) that are willing to put money into large-scale infrastructure projects in developing nations.
Part Three: Enabling Questions	Participant Responses

Barriers and roadblocks: What are the existing barriers (local, governmental, political, defense, cultural, etc) that need to be overcome by the adversary to bring about the threat? How to these barriers and roadblocks differ geographically? How could the operating environment change to be more beneficial to them?	• Lack of Understanding. It is difficult for William to explain the threat because he is not an SME. Also, Kirsten cannot convincingly communicate the potential of the threat to her superiors for the same reason. Separately, William is met with resistance from the publishing industry because it too does not fully understand/imagine what 'could be.' The perceived threat "AI-created images are leveraged to further China's goal to share the *fruits of development*" is hard to comprehend because it's never been done before and there are too many reasons NOT to believe it.
	• Organizational Structures and Inter- Intra- organizational sharing. William presents what he's learned (as a journalist unincumbered by any kind of structure) to Kirsten (as a low-level financial crimes investigator that must adhere to laws, protocols, leadership decisions, public accountability, risk-versus-reward, etc). Government organizations are not always structured – or have the capacity – to investigate a threat or commit limited resources to something:
	    a) that has not happened yet, and
	    b) involves multiple innovations/methods that have not been seen before.

What industry (or industries) are impacted? Who stands to gain and who stands to lose?	• Publishing Industry being used as an unwitting partner – not knowing they are printing industrial espionage. • Nations in agreement with "fair" global development or in receipt of stolen technology (Does BRICS become a 'new center of international power and influence?') • Hegemony of highly industrialized nations and the profits of privatization (protected intellectual property) of multi-billion-dollar infrastructure projects.

Fig. 4.5 Experiential and enabling prompts and the participant responses

Part Four: Backcasting	Participant Responses
What could bring this future about? What is different in ten years?	• China's continued economic and development expansion. • Developments in AI. • Increased knowledge gap between AI development and regulatory and/or law enforcement. • Continued threats to investigative journalists.
What changes in policy or regulatory bodies might need to happen?	• The United Nations aligning/supporting BRICS as other 'western nations' display apathy towards the MDGs and SDGs. • Right now (2025) only the EU has attempted to build meaningful AI regulations. If they can be upheld in court (which remains to be seen) other nations will follow suit.
What new technologies need to be made?	• The technology to develop large-scale development projects that physically connect two continents. • Continued development in Artificial Intelligence (or the understanding that it could do what Kittle says it can do now)

Fig. 4.6 Backcasting prompts and participant responses

Unlike other models, Threatcasting includes interventions as part of the process. Typically, when a strategic planning model is deployed—where participant design a plausible future world—the implications and recovery are done by analysts or leaders after the workshop has concluded. Here, however, participants not only define what is possible, but also "what needs to happen in disrupt, mitigate, and prevent it" from coming to fruition [18]. Here too, we see an opportunity to apply human-centric design to the recovery, see Fig. 4.6.

4.3 Storycasting Model: The Three-Act Play

Threatcasting participants provide a skeleton of a story. Key plot points, basic character development, locations, and a sequence of events. This summary, or **schema**, is a framework that organizes information and makes sense of their plausible future world. In the context of storytelling, a schema is instrumental in outlining a cohesive and engaging narrative for Storycasting. It serves as our blueprint to the progression of events and whatever evolves into the novel threat out there on the ten-year horizon. Additionally, a well-defined schema helps writers maintain focus on key elements without wandering off into the tangents.

Participants are encouraged to give each of the scenarios a catchy title—though I wonder if this would happen naturally without any encouragement. This helps clarify the theme and tone of the future scenario. This scenario includes novel applications of AI, geopolitics, law enforcement's understanding of a yet-to-be discovered crime and involves *the person* at the center of the story, William Kittle. The title could also provide a clue as to what the participants think is the most compelling part of their scenario. Should this be a story about a person? Should the plot focus on the novel threat? Should the story emphasize the risks of a technology or to a particular industry domain? If so, which industry?

Participant responses provided in Figs. 4.4, 4.5 and 4.6, involve a European law enforcement agency, an industrial construction corporation, the United Nations, China, and tangentially, the publishing industry. The focus of the story is for the participants to decide, but I also think the writer or creator of the writing project should weigh some options as well. Sometimes it can take a while to settle on a title, and there is often fun involved in that as well. Here are some title ideas for our simulated data:

Hack-GPT
The Curious Case of Kittle
Lost In Translation
HokkenStrutt's Hack
The UN and BRICS Alliance
Bridge to the Future

For the following demonstration, not only will we use the participant responses to the prompts listed in Figs. 4.4, 4.5 and 4.6, but also the title the imaginary participants provided. For the remainder of this process, I've chosen the title *Lost in Translation* because it is a clever play on words. It reflects the novel use of AI writing, but also the inability of the main characters and law enforcement or government organizations to understand a threat that has not happened yet. It's catchy and thought-provoking.

To make the transition from plausible to compelling a little easier, we can use a template. The Three-Act Play and Five-Act Play models are a classic structure commonly used in storytelling, particularly in plays, screenplays, and novels. It has been around since the fourth century and is used widely in all forms of storytelling, from television shows to novels. It divides a plot—or story—into distinct parts, each serving a specific purpose in advancing the plot and character development. Information and explanations about the Three- and Five-Act Play can be found in many places; however for *Storycasting*, John Yorke's *Into the Woods* [19] is helpful. For *Storycasting*, the Three-Act Play works well because the Threatcasting methodology emulates it almost perfectly. While the Five-Act Play model is included for reference for *Storycasting*, the Three-Act Play is sufficient, see Fig. 4.7.

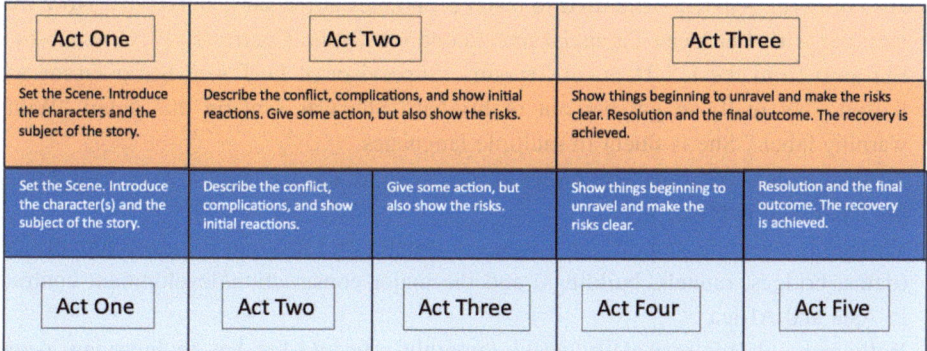

Fig. 4.7 Simple visualization of the three- and five-act play as described by the author

4.4 Inserting Participant Responses into the Three-Act Play Template

The Three-Act Play format provides prompts as to where Threatcasting participant replies would best fit. For instance, many of the datapoints provided in Part One: Who is your Person (Fig. 4.4) provide the basic framing of the characters and can be included in Act One. The replies found in Part Two: Experience Questions and Part Three: Enabling Questions (Fig. 4.5) can be moved around in any of the three acts as you decide how and when you want to reveal them to the reader. Again, this can take some time and creativity. Lastly, the participant responses to Part Four: Backcasting (Fig. 4.6) easily fit in Act Three, where the story's resolution and the characters and organizations seek to build resilience to the novel threats.

After reviewing each reply or datapoint provided by the participants, I inserted them into one of the three acts. We do not have the story yet, but we have the key plot points and can start to envision where we want them. This helps frame the plot and would likely involve some adjustments as the story is written. Below is how I took the qualitative data and imagined where they would best fit into the Three-Act Play format. This, in practice, helps frame or draft initial storytelling and can be adjusted as the writing continues.

Act One: **Set the Scene. Introduce the Character(s) and the Subject of the Story**.

- William Kittle. He's a 30+ year-old African American. Tall and out of shape. Since his divorce (short marriage no kids) not much of a personal life outside of his work.
- William is a writer who quit his job teaching International Relations at a midwestern state university to write full-time. He's been published in *The Atlantic, Wired* and others.

- His colleague Kirsten—she used to teach economics at the same university. Now she's working with European Financial and Economic Crime Centre (EFECC, a subset of Europol) from the US Dept. of Treasury. Supervisor at DoT sent her overseas as a liaison—but really to get her out of his hair. She was sent on this detail "With a warning label." She is fluent in multiple languages.
- William lives a vagabond life but currently living in the UK with a work visa through his UK-based publisher/agent.
- William is currently working on a series of articles on European Infrastructure projects (dams, bridges, tunnels, buildings) and the major construction/development contracts in Asia and Africa.
- William builds his own daily/weekly/monthly schedule but has to interview people in various industries. Think: Robert Young Pelton meets Tom Woodward, but not as charismatic.
- William is doing the legwork for a larger piece of investigative journalism about new EU/China and EU/Africa infrastructure projects. He is at an interview with an industrial company when he "accidentally" takes a stack of papers off the floor. This includes an internal memo that suggests there is an AI-powered imaging program capable of hiding technical information in other digital documents—online journals, public-facing websites, e-books, etc.

Act Two: **Describe the Conflict, Complications, and Show Initial Reactions. Give Some Action but also Show the Risks**.

- His publishing agent, Andrea. She promotes/supports William's work.
- Other people in William's community are other writers like him, academics, publishing professionals—and for the purposes of this scenario—SMEs he interviews for his writing project(s).
- China's continued economic and development expansion.
- The technology to develop large-scale development projects that physically connect two continents.
- William surreptitiously (and not exactly honestly) gets ahold of information from a German construction company, that they a) knew their industrial design databases were hacked, and b) China was going to back out of a multi-billion-dollar construction deal. Both of these pieces of information—the company fears—will ruin the company's future and will make them responsible for weakening future EU-centric infrastructure deals and East/West political impacts.
- After working on the story some more, William presents what he's learned to his colleague, Kirsten.
- Until he gets something published, he's not making any money, though he may get some up-front funding from publishers if they accept his book proposal.
- He is beholden to his agent who promotes his work.

4.4 Inserting Participant Responses into the Three-Act Play Template 55

- An unknown group of hackers.
- Unknown industrial leaders from China, South Africa, and Brazil.
- An unknown group of 'supporters' from the UN.
- Kirsten believes there is credibility to what William shares; however when Kirsten presents her initial findings to Senior Leadership at EFECC, their reactions reflect skepticism, archaic organizational structures, and unwillingness to risk resources investigating a novel crime that has not yet been committed.
- Lack of Understanding. It is difficult for William to explain the threat because he is not an SME. Also, Kirsten cannot convincingly communicate the potential of the threat to her superiors for the same reason. Separately, William is met with resistance from the publishing industry because it too does not fully understand/imagine what 'could be.' The perceived threat "AI-created images are leveraged to further China's goal to share the *fruits of development*" is hard to comprehend because it's never been done before and there are too many reasons NOT to believe it.

Act Three: **Show Things Beginning to Unravel and Make the Risks Clear. Resolution and the Final Outcome. The Recovery is Achieved**.

- Continued threats to investigative journalists.
- If EFECC does not take the novel threat seriously, he would be compelled to write an article about how they were incapable/unwilling to investigate.
- Because the laws/norms/applications of AI are still being developed, understanding how it could be a threat is complex. For this scenario there are a few potential threats:
- A threat to the status quo: China, a key member of BRICS, is seeking to develop the whole of the world 'equally and fairly'—the whole of humanity, not just the 'first world.' IMF, NATO, World Bank, EU and all the G7-through-G20s may not believe/trust/support China's intentions.
- After publishing a few articles about what he's learned, Kittle dies under mysterious circumstances. A threat to journalists: 2023 was deadly for journalists, and the lack of trust in journalism/news as a whole is on the rise. If they are to continue to be a part of the news/information (free press, unfettered journalism) and relied upon to find/report what's going on behind the scenes in geopolitics, industrial development, global partnerships) will they become targets? Will the job of a journalist go away? Will journalists be barred from certain countries?
- Investigative and Regulatory Bodies: As older generations of senior leaders retire, will the traditional model of 'workers only work as directed and only leaders make decisions' change? If a junior financial investigator is not empowered to pursue a novel threat, will they leave that industry and move elsewhere? (like the white-hat hacker becoming a black-hat hacker)
- Organizational Structures and Inter-Intra-organizational sharing. William presents what he's learned (as a journalist unencumbered by any kind of structure) to Kirsten (as a

low-level financial crimes investigator that must adhere to laws, protocols, leadership decisions, public accountability, risk-versus-reward, etc.). Government organizations are not always structured—or have the capacity—to investigate a threat or commit limited resources to something:

(a) that has not happened yet, and
(b) involves multiple innovations/methods that have not been seen before.

- IMF and the World Bank may find a Rising China is inevitable but cannot politically support their goals.
- As the UN is struggling to achieve its Millennium Development Goals, it may find itself an ally to BRICS nations (current and pending members).
- Publishing Industry being used as an unwitting partner—not knowing they are printing industrial espionage.
- Nations in agreement with "fair" global development or in receipt of stolen technology (Does BRICS become a 'new center of international power and influence?)
- Hegemony of highly industrialized nations and the profits of privatization (protected intellectual property) of multi-billion-dollar infrastructure projects.
- Increased knowledge gap between AI development and regulatory and/or law enforcement.
- The United Nations aligning/supporting BRICS as other 'western nations' display apathy toward the MDGs and SDGs.
- Right now (2025) only the EU has attempted to build meaningful AI regulations. If they can be upheld in court (which remains to be seen), other nations will follow suit.

Now the real creativity begins. More tools for writing will be covered later, but I will demonstrate how I took the above data and turned it into a short story. While other options are possible and involve far less work, it made more sense to complete the principal—or largest—writing option first and then adapt it to the smaller formats later. In the next pages you will find, in under ten thousand words, an example of converting participant replies into a compelling story.

4.5 Storycasting Model: A Compelling Story

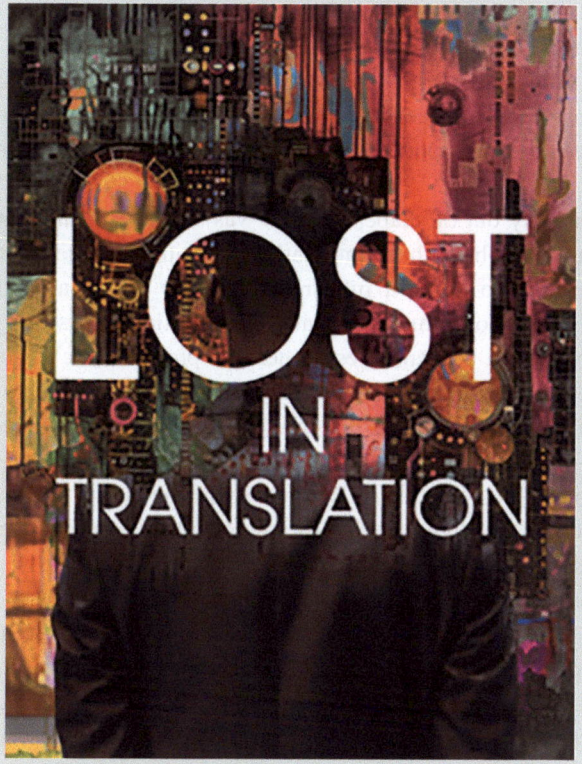

Lost in Translation

A Storycasting original by Christopher Owens

Created with data from (NAME OF WORKSHOP) Threatcasting Workshop on (DATE)

Source content provided by (NAME OF COHORT)

Act One:
January 15, 2034

William Kittle was sitting patiently in the lobby of The HokkenStrutt Corporation's German headquarters. As he waited, he read an article about the rising violence against journalists. It included a graph that showed the number journalists imprisoned or killed across the globe had skyrocketed in the previous five years. *Not a smart career move,* he thought to himself. For a decade, HokkenStrutt's ongoing large-scale construction contracts in South America and Southeast Asia made it one of the fastest growing companies in Europe. That is exactly why William needed the interview.

"Someone will be with you in a moment," the woman at the front desk quietly announced. She was kind enough to speak in English, not wanting him to construct another sentence in his rusty high school level German. William felt out of place while travelling Germany. Yes, he'd seen other black men and woman, but not another African American. Not even at the airport. He still needed to get used to his new life with new rhythms.

Tall and increasingly out of shape, William was still recovering from divorce. As the dust settled, he quit his job teaching International Relations at the University of Chicago and committed himself to being a full-time writer. Or was it a journalist? He wasn't sure what title to bestow on himself at that point. Within the first six months, using his credentials as a published academic researcher and professor, he'd gotten a few articles picked up by a few credible online outlets, most notably, *The Atlantic,* and *Wired.*

A month earlier, just before the holidays, he'd successfully pitched the idea for a book that would—at least academically—answer the question "How is China going to economically expand in the world?" William spent the week cold-calling and knocking on doors—literally and figuratively—to arrange interviews before his money ran out. He'd received a small stipend, arranged by his publicist, Andrea. His initial interviews with policy makers, economists, and corporations could have led to a series of separate articles. Or, if he collected enough material, some chapters in a non-fiction book on global development projects. He focused on infrastructure projects—dams, bridges, tunnels, railways—and their major development contracts in Asia and Africa.

A grounded pragmatist, William never distracted himself when researching geopolitical issues. He was intrigued by a presentation on China's global development goals for 2035. That too, was an additional element to his research. "Do you really believe China is that altruistic?" a fellow professor asked him at his farewell luncheon back in Chicago. "They want Africa's resources. They will exploit Africans, not be their savior. How can you not see that?" he later bellowed at William. Maybe it was ironic that an African American wouldn't see it that way, but that was not how William approached his work: Write what you learn, not what you feel about what you learn. He'd never write an op-ed piece if he could help it.

The receptionist noticed William looking at his watch again. It had been twenty minutes. If she was hoping he'd give up, she was wrong. His flight wasn't leaving for six days. He had the tenacity to wait until his money ran out.

Five minutes later he was met with a handshake and a public relations smile, "Good morning, Herr Kittle, my name is Greta Ruckert." Her accent revealed she learned English in a British boarding school. She walked him into her office without another word.

4.5 Storycasting Model: A Compelling Story

William went through the interview asking typical questions about the company and previous industrial projects. Greta answered the questions like she was pitching the company to a room of investors. She repeated the company's vision to be a "Leader in European economic partnership across the Middle East, and Southeast Asia," just as it was written on their website. That was the opening William was looking for. He inquired about the upcoming bridge project with China.

"Did you not see the news yesterday?" she asked with a raised eyebrow suggesting he hadn't done his research. He silently nodded yes. She was terse and sterile, "Our company put out a press release." She handed William a copy of a one-pager. He quickly scanned it as Greta spoke. It stated China suddenly backed out of 10-year deal worth billions. She added, "This is very upsetting, and our legal team is pursuing what fines or sanction can be brought against them."

William hadn't seen the news, "No, I understand this," he bluffed. "What I mean is, why did they do that? This was potentially going to be the longest bridge in the world, wasn't it? Your company developed new ocean-bottom construction techniques? And some kind of proprietary concrete? The sandy ocean bottom and length of span required proprietary HokkenStrutt engineering, I thought."

Sitting back in her chair, Greta pointed to the paper in William's hands, "Hokken-Strutt's position is in the press release." She added, "There will be another statement later today. It will explain both the German government and HokkenStrutt have significant economic and political influence to leverage against their dishonoring the contract."

William had been quietly holding one last card. Sensing that the interview was ending abruptly, he played his last hand. "I'd like to ask you about the ransomware attack last month, if you have a moment."

Greta stood up from her chair, gesturing for him to remain seated. "I cannot discuss that. I do not work in that department." It was clear that Greta didn't expect William would know about it. Because HokkenStrutt managed their public communications and security so well, Greta knew there were very few people outside the company aware of the attack. They had even not told their stockholders, in fact. William's three contacts in the murky world of cybersecurity were more helpful in preparation for this interview than she'd assumed.

"Did I get bad information?" William asked in an attempt to disarm Greta.

"Wait here please. I will be right back." Without further conversation, Greta walked out. William sat in a chair against the wall, across from Greta's desk in her office. He noticed a small stack of folders in a box under the chair next to his. Casually, he looked to see if anyone in the hallway could see him. He used a few fingers to flip some pages in the top folder. From his seat he noticed some key phrases and page headers that stunned him. He saw a CD in a plastic sleeve. *Who still has a computer with a CD driver?* Then he did something even he didn't expect. It took just a second. When done. he sat quietly, waiting for her to return. The CD was now squirrelled in his hand.

Greta startled him, "Please come with me," motioning to the things in William's hands which had the press release she gave him on top, "and take that with you." She didn't notice that William continued to hold the small stack of papers and the CD under the press release. *She told me to take it with me*, he rationalized.

Walking briskly through the hallway of the corporate headquarters, she spoke hastily, announcing that she was needed in a meeting. Ending with, "If you would like to speak with someone at HokkenStrutt about any other topics, I suggest you call the same number you called for this interview."

The halls were glass and concrete, offering dull echoes of muted office conversations. He could sense the tension in the offices around him. Before William could muster another question, he found himself back in the lobby being shown the door.

January 17, 2034

William drove all the way to The Hague from Germany just to meet with his former colleague, Kirsten. She'd left her position in the University of Chicago teaching economics a year before William. She was offered a job with the Treasury Department in Washington, DC, but soon found she didn't quite fit the mold as a Financial Crime Investigator. Without warning, her supervisor sent her an email with a position description for a liaison position at the European Financial and Economic Crime Center (EFECC) in The Hague. Her lackluster performance combined with her teaching background and fluency in six languages led to her receiving a "strong recommendation to develop liaison skills overseas" from her immediate supervisor. For the past three months, she'd been assigned to the Expertise and Stakeholder Management Unit, putting together training materials on financial crimes. She was back to teaching again. Monotonous work, but she was exceptionally good at it.

"So great to see you, William," she began as they took a seat at a bench in Westduinpark. She asked only half joking, "I heard you left Chicago right after the divorce to be a writer or something. Mid-life crisis or a fresh start?"

"A little of both," he sheepishly admitted. "Thanks for meeting with me on short notice. I didn't know who else to turn to."

Sipping her latte, "That sounds ominous, William."

"Well, I'm not in over my head, but I think I've uncovered something," William began. He explained the project he'd begun and his recent interviews at five corporations, ending with his meeting at HokkenStrutt.

Kirsten knew, of course, all about the Chinese backing out of the deal. The implications on EU relations with China and the financial strain this would cause HokkenStrutt were significant. William added that they'd already invested millions fabricating the infrastructure needed to build a first-of-its-kind bridge. Further, because this construction was going to be done in China, HokkenStrutt already began the expensive process of designing the

4.5 Storycasting Model: A Compelling Story

construction site on the other side of the globe. After they ensuring they had a shared understanding of the scenario, Kirsten asked, "So what's got you tied up in knots?".

"When I was in HokkenStrutt's offices, I asked about a cyberattack they'd experienced."

Kirsten shrugged her shoulders, "I hadn't heard about that, but that's not really my specialty."

"Well even if it was, you likely wouldn't have heard about it," William assured her, "I only knew about it through some shady friends who know about hacking and the dark web and all the other things that go bump in the night. This brings me to my other point," William shifted nervously on the park bench they shared. He looked over his shoulder subconsciously.

"Oh my gawd, you're so dramatic," Kirsten teased.

William's face never lightened, "I accidentally left their corporate offices with some company papers and a CD."

She didn't believe 'accidentally' was true, but also didn't push the issue. Then Kirsten cocked her head to the side at the thought of getting information off a CD.

Knowing what she was thinking, he added "I had to buy an external CD driver online. And it was in German, so I'm struggling to decipher everything. Long story short; someone at HokkenStrutt was doing some internal damage control after the cyberattack." William was able to gather a few names and details from the digital documents, but in a few instances, it sounded like he was forcing connections between detached bits of information.

Regardless of her first impressions, Kirsten was transfixed as William continued. Then stopped him, "I have to be honest, William, this is not really my domain. This sounds like cybercrime. Why did you think to share this with me?".

"Well, I'm certain that a crime has occurred. They are too." He continued with more fragmented information he'd gathered. They continued talking for twenty minutes before they got up from the park bench. "Who would investigate something like this?" William asked.

Walking across the park, they talked more about diagrams and drawings William saw on the documents. Kirsten told William she would ask around the EFECC offices. "I barely know how our organization chart works." She laughed with a bit of frustration, "and I'm not sure this is something that the EFECC would investigate." Kirsten explained that the EFECC was a subset of Europol, and jurisdictional lines were complex. Adding to the complication, Kirsten was only serving as a liaison from the Treasury Department. Also, both William and Kirsten were US citizens, "So I don't know what my official reporting responsibility is in this case," Kirsten added. "What are your intentions? I mean, what are you going to do with this information?".

It was clear William had already thought through a lot of this. "I'm in an agreement to research and write. I have a contract of sorts, to write about what my stipend is supporting," he began. "So yeah, I am going to write about this. I have no reason to exclude what I know. My publicist is going to go nuts over this."

Kirsten asked cautiously, "What do you mean?" not knowing if 'nuts' was a good thing or a bad thing.

"This might be a huge story. No, it *is* a huge story. I already have enough to write an article. An article that would get picked up very quickly, I might add. I want to sit on it and get some more information off the CD." William looked at Kirsten for a moment, "I don't think I should tell anyone that I've spoken to you specifically, or where you work," cautiously he hinted, "but it would be interesting to know what the EFECC or Europol or Interpol thinks about all this." William realized that while he felt like he was over his head, Kirsten was definitely out of her comfort zone, not even sure what her responsibilities were.

Kirsten and William made a tentative agreement. She would do some cautious digging at the EFECC. William would present information about the HokkenStrutt interview to his publicist but would leave out specifics of Kirsten and the EFECC. Also, he would continue to investigate more into the failed construction project. Kirsten and William would have to be careful. For each of them, the developments they were about to share with their colleagues could be the biggest breakthrough in their new careers or it could be what brings an early end to their new careers.

Act Two:
February 1, 2034

"Get in here, William," he heard through the open door. William exchanged an eye roll with Andrea's assistant, Gloria. Born in Nigeria, Andrea had lived throughout the UK for the past four decades working first as a newspaper reporter in the late nineties. In 2024 she sensed the demise of print writing was inevitable and focused on digital publishing and writers across Europe. Based in Manchester, England, Andrea had been William's publishing agent since he committed to a full-time writing career. Experienced and driven, she loved writers like William because they knew their careers were on the line with every assignment. William gave Andrea a quick readout of three articles he'd been outlining.

He pitched each one as Andrea typed her notes, offering a polite "Mm Hmm" every so often. "Ok. Those all sound fit. I'll send out some emails and see who might be interested in them. Keep me up to date." Andrea looked up from the computer screen, "Tell me how you are using that stipend. The interviews in Germany went well? You said in your email you spoke with five companies or something like that." She tried to recall the details he'd sent a few days ago when they scheduled this meeting, "And there's something special

4.5 Storycasting Model: A Compelling Story

about a bridge contract? What is going on with that?" Andrea suspected William was going to ask for more money to up-front his travel.

"Yes, HokkenStrutt in Berlin. I tried to get a second visit, but they didn't return my calls after my first meeting with the bulldog running their public relations department." William already had a document open on his laptop prepared with bullet points to keep him on-task with Andrea. He gave her a ten-minute summary of the work HokkenStrutt specializes in, their significant position in the EU economic system, their global reach, and their expansion goals in the Far East and Middle East regions. "They are directly competing with firms of equal size and reach. Their main competitors come from companies in India, Russia, and China." William wasn't sure how much Andrea understood about the growing influence of BRICS, but also didn't want to get caught mansplaining either.

"And what's the problem?" Andrea was looking for the point that William was obviously leading her to.

After fidgeting a bit in his chair, William sat up strait. He continued, putting his laptop aside and took a sip of the incredibly strong coffee, "The day before I got there, China backed out of a huge construction deal with HokkenStrutt. By some measures, it was going to be significant. I dunno, maybe the longest single span, or the longest in total length. Something like that. Anyway, we're talking about hundreds of billions of Euro and a decade of work in China. Lots of jobs created too. It was heralded as a windfall in EU and China economic partnerships. Lots of other industries saw this as a precedent for other economic deals. Biomedical companies, agricultural projects, and a general easing of relations between the East and West." William paused for another sip of coffee and wondered if he was overselling or underselling the scope of things. Andrea sat calmly, waiting for William to drop the other shoe. "HokkenStrutt is going to lean on the EU to fight it somehow—however those things get fought." He wanted to focus on the impacts, not his own conjecture, "This is a big deal, Andrea. They have already spent millions building infrastructure. I did a little digging and asking around; the corporation is in financial trouble if they can't get China to honor the deal."

William paused. He wasn't sure if he should tell Andrea everything. The CD he obtained from the HokkenStrutt office had a lot more information about their financials and the cyberattack, but he wasn't sure how Andrea would react to his shenanigans. Andrea began asking questions about the interview and what else he thought he could learn from a second interview—if they'd answer his calls and emails. Without his asking, Andrea weakly offered to "find some funding" if he used it only for this specific story, but she didn't sound very convincing.

He said nothing about the CD to Andrea. He left her office feeling uneasy.

February 20, 2034

William flew back to Germany and scheduled interviews for his article on EU and Chinese economic partnerships. He spent more time in person, on the phone, and via Zoom with more economists, policymakers, and corporate offices.

In between, William made some calls to other journalists and reporters he'd cultivated as colleagues. He asked, cautiously and vaguely, if they'd ever used physical information they'd obtained accidentally. The responses they offered were equally as cautious and vague. One war reporter who'd been imbedded with British SAS in the late stages of the Second Gulf War said with a smirk, "Someone imbedded with British SAS once told me they used information they found in a desk drawer when they were looking for a pen. Some documents outlined how Iraq was funding the Taliban." Another writer admitted to using information they'd found in a hotel lobby as "unsubstantiated but reliable information they'd obtained first-hand." They all suggested his only recourse was to reach out to HokkenStrutt and see if someone can corroborate the information.

He repeated emails and calls asking them to respond to "unsubstantiated but reliable information regarding the loss of proprietary design data and construction techniques through a cyberattack." They still weren't responding to his requests to speak with him.

It was too tedious for him to translate large sections of German documents, even using his computer and translation tools. William had made a few calls and made a copy for someone he could trust to discretely translate the German technical documents on the CD into English. That too, would cost money which William struggled to accumulate.

Within a few days, William received an email from his translator. There was more information about China. They met in person, avoiding any digital footprint, and William collected the copy from his translator. This new information gave William a broader scope and scale for the story, but he wanted to see how far Kirsten got with her financial crimes collogues. He called her right away.

March 1, 2034

As soon as they met, Kirsten started. "Honestly, this is a non-starter on my end, William. I spoke to a few people and asked around, just trying to get a sense of who I should talk to at the EFECC."

"And? No one is interested?" William sounded deflated.

"There's really nothing to be interested in. China backed out of a huge construction deal with a German company. That is not out of the ordinary in 2034. Lots of international deals fall through. If there's a crime, it's not a financial crime. At least not one the EFECC or Europol would be interested in. Sorry, buddy."

Kirsten was too embarrassed to tell him that part of the problem is that no one at the EFECC took *her* seriously. She was a former economics professor who was now financial crimes investigator from the US who was sent off to Europe to write training manuals. Worse, there was a 'Caution Tag' hanging around her neck when she arrived based on some poor performance reviews. She didn't have enough time in the law enforcement community to be considered 'experienced' and despite her mastery of languages, she was unable to communicate the potential magnitude of a crime that had not been reported by HokkenStrutt. At that point Kirsten was feeling self-conscious that she got caught up in William's journalistic fantasy. Further, she was a bit dubious about information found on a CD that might be stolen property. "Is there anything of substance in the CD?".

William pulled open a leather courier bag he kept strapped across his chest even as they sat at the café. He pulled out some notes from his translator—never admitting to Kirsten he used a translator—and started to reveal new information. "HokkenStrutt knew that the attack was focused on their digital databases. There was no evidence that emails or financials or anything related to contracts were stolen or corrupted. I didn't find any specific date, but someone at HokkenStrutt wrote an internal report showing that all of the design specs, engineering, and everything else they'd developed for the bridge in China was copied off their servers. Lots of the technical language in the report—well, there are a few reports actually—is a bit over my head, but they knew their proprietary engineering was taken. Or copied. They know someone else has it." William continued for another ten minutes with more information he'd found in the files he'd obtained. Kirsten waited a few more minutes before William stopped to catch his breath.

"Still. This sounds like cybercrime, not financial crime," Kirsten offered.

William pressed, "It's more than that. It's international crime. It's corporate crime. Isn't that financial crime?".

"Ok, but to what end? What is the goal of the theft? Who stole it? What are they going to do with the data; sell it on the dark web? The dark web is monitored as much as the regular web. Nothing digital is truly hidden any longer." She added, "No one secretly builds a bridge that big." Kirsten was trying to be helpful, but she couldn't risk too much for a half-assumed international corporate crime that hadn't happened yet. "Look, I see it like this." She paused to make sure she didn't sound dismissive, "There's only a theoretical crime. If what you say is true, then a cybercrime has occurred. We can agree on that. It was not reported, however. Until that stolen material is sold—meaning that the actual proprietary information is found to be in the possession of someone other than HokkenStrutt—there is no role for government to act—regulatory or enforcement."

William sat quietly. Frozen, holding a half dozen pages in each hand. Kirsten made an excellent point. Stealing proprietary technical information is not enough of a story. Proprietary information also needs to be transmitted. It needs to be shared or sold. He thought more about what was translated on the CD and in the papers. Now William was the one feeling embarrassed. He thought about his next move. "I have a meeting with some nefarious friends. Here in Europe. I asked them to see if they could find out anything for me. They called me the next day they said they wanted to meet me in person."

"What about?" Kirsten was cautious.

"They wouldn't tell me, exactly." He lowered his voice, "They said they could share with me some information they'd found. They were elusive, as people like them tend to be, but suggested that I read a document from 2021 put out by China. In it, China defines their global development plans." William pulled out another set of stapled pages and handed it to Kirsten. "Here, you can keep this copy. I found it online. It's not a secret document or anything. It's in the public domain," he assured her.

"Ok. And?" Kirsten flipped through the document just to amuse him. Kirsten was visibly irritated.

William went on a five-minute summation of his theories and ideas, but saw Kirsten was no longer following him. He finished his thought anyway, "My guy says that he can give me proof that China has—and I'm quoting him here—political support from global leaders to expand development projects across the globe. He also says he thinks he knows how technical information can be shared with only the intended recipients. Something about an AI-created digital image used like a one-time key code." They stared at each other for a second. He was thinking about big implications. William was also thinking about the money he was going to pay his snoop for the information. William's bank account was thinning by the week.

Kirsten and William finished their lattes in awkward silence. He put away his papers. Kirsten didn't buy what William was telling her, but also thought this was more interesting than writing financial crimes training. She would continue to accommodate this little distraction, if for no other reason than to entertain herself.

"I'll ask around again," was all she could offer.

March 29, 2034

Kirsten sat at her desk pouring through source materials to use in a new training curriculum for a course called *The Future of Cyber Enabled Crime*. She'd been asked a few weeks back to research content to put into the course. She sat back from her computer screen to rub her temples and close her eyes for a moment.

"Sorry to wake you," Gunter began with his sarcastic tone, "but I heard you were asking about China's development goals and European overseas construction contracts."

In his mid-thirties, Gunter was bright, but infamously and incredibly off-putting in his demeanor. Gunter's reputation was, aside from his Austrian accent, that he spoke in a unique dialect of condescension and a total lack of curiosity in what anyone else thinks or knows about a topic. Despite this reputation, Kirsten attempted to join the conversation, "Yes, well not exactly. I was approached by someone…".

"Well, I told a few people I would come over and help you out. You are probably not aware, but in 2021 China put out a document that explains their approach to global development. I'll email you a link so you can get up to speed on that. Also, I do not think that someone who teaches financial crime is the right person to be asking our financial crimes leadership about German industrial contracts." Gunter continued to lecture Kirsten

4.5 Storycasting Model: A Compelling Story

without pause for another five minutes at least. She listened quietly, waiting for him to catch his breath between sentences and declarations and assumptions. He did not.

What Kirsten pieced together from Gunter was that two weeks earlier—when she visited one of the offices in the financial crimes division—and mentioned that she was approached by an American journalist, the story must have been told and retold and slowly transformed into office gossip. At one point he added dismissively, "I do not have the time to explain the current trends in cyberattacks, but I can email you some things on that too, I guess."

As Kirsten continued to listen, Gunter eventually and inadvertently revealed that by the time the story got to him, it had somehow changed suggesting Kirsten was asking for an article to be written—not that someone was research an article already. "If you stay here long enough, you will understand how we do things. I have to go, email me if you have any more questions. I will let them know you understand what I have explained."

Gunter walked away as tersely as he arrived at her desk ten minutes earlier. Kirsten had barely spoken a word. She returned to rubbing her eyes. Within minutes she received an email. Gunter copied her on an unsolicited message to Kirsten's supervisor, his supervisor, and three others that he'd "helped her understand her role," and ended with "I will provide her more guidance on financial matters, cybercrime, and reporting procedures only as they apply to her role as a training developer." His email and visit to her desk left her feeling embarrassed that she failed to effectively communicate what she felt was a credible source reporting information about a theoretical crime. Although she'd been dismissive to William, she thought he was on to something.

April 2, 2034

Despite the growing humiliation Kirsten felt, she begrudgingly agreed to meet William again. Because he was already in the area, they'd arranged to meet at a restaurant near her office in The Hague. As soon as they sat down, she could see William was filled with angst.

"I know you don't want me to come to you with this anymore," William began. "But I've been doing research on this and it's becoming more compelling."

"William, please understand, this isn't something I'm in the position to be a part of." Kirsten was still feeling the sting from being chastised. Marlene Harlow, the Training Manager, summoned Kirsten in her office to explain the details of her initial interactions with William, what he explained to Kirsten, and how she felt it applied to her role as a training content creator. Ultimately, Kirsten was instructed to write a document summarizing everything William told her in their discussion. Marlene said, "After I read your report, I'll consider what the appropriate actions—if any—should be taken by the EFECC."

Kirsten was hesitant to explain any of this in detail to William for a few reasons. First, she wasn't sure William would appreciate the structures found within law enforcement agencies. The complicated and hidden world of cybercrime was well beyond his understanding. Because he could not explain things clearly and with any certainty to Kirsten, she in turn, could not articulate the threat. Lastly, Kirsten feared that William would include their interactions in something he would inevitably write. An article on the internet? Some kind of exposé in *The New Yorker*? Or worse; he might write a full-length piece of non-fiction.

Kirsten's attention was returned to the small café table when William spoke again. "Kirsten there's more to this than I imagined. I paid a few people to do some digital searching for me." He paused to see if Kirsten heard his inference to about black hat hackers and the Dark Web and other forms of information gathering. She did not.

William placed some papers in front of Kirsten. "There's more in here about AI-created images too. I don't quite understand it yet, but…" He chose his next words carefully, "This guy I know, he said that it's possible that China is going to publish HokkenStutt's designs. So, anyone can have them." Kirsten looked at him curiously. He continued cautiously, "It's likely they'll use AI to layer the technical data—the designs and diagrams and specs—in other digitally-created images. Then anyone who knows where to look for them can replicate them. Maybe China will build the bridge themselves, or maybe one between Yemen or Djibouti. Or India or one of the other BRICS nations will get the contract worth billions."

Kirsten was starting to envision William sitting in a dark room wearing a tin foil hat. He continued, "I have to clear it with my publisher before I write it, but there is a connection to the United Nations."

"I don't follow," Kirsten was eating and only half listening. "Wait, United Nations? What are you talking about?"

Again, William went on a tear. Kirsten could barely keep up. At one point he was talking about the United Nations Millennium Development Goals, then back to Hokken-Stutt's data being stolen, then human development and The Silk Road initiative. Kirsten was flipping through a printout he'd handed her. Brightly colored blocks on a page that looked like a well-designed marketing proposal. She'd heard of the MDGs and knew they were filled with all the typical phrases about food security, human rights, and basic human needs. In the middle of the one-pager, she read a quote from UN Secretary-General. Kirsten read it aloud, nodding her head in acknowledgement of what she was reading, "Yes, these are a 'to-do list for people and the planet.' So what?" Kirsten stared at William with a blank face.

"Kirsten, really? You don't see this? This is a significant shift in global influence. This is a major shift in soft power. Economic power." William implored, "This isn't just about stealing proprietary design information from a European company. It's way bigger."

Kirsten found herself getting caught up in everything William was saying. On the table in front of her, she noticed he'd placed more papers without her realizing. She flipped through them. they looked like printouts from some online servers though she couldn't be sure. One document was an internal email from someone at the International

Monetary Fund who, based on what Kirsten could follow, sounded even more paranoid than William. The email used phrases like "a direct challenge to long-held centers of economic influence" and "increased desire for nations to join economic alliances and trade with BRICS." Again, Kirsten felt she was out of her depth, but continued to scan the papers William placed in front of her.

After a few moments of silence, Kirsten looked up at William, "So what are you going to do?" She was afraid of his answer.

"I have a story here. There is no doubt. I can't show you everything I have." Much of his information was obtained through methods not available to law enforcement agencies. Journalists and writers, however, work in a vastly different domain and with different methods. "I will continue to write this story, but…"

"But what?"

"My publisher is not interested in me putting out a book yet." He paused, "She wants me to put together an article she can put in front of people at places like *The Guardian*, or *Wired,* or maybe *The Economist.* But that too has risks. Because…"

"What?"

"Because I told her I've tipped off someone at the EFECC."

Kirsten's face went blank.

William assured her, "I'm not required to name my sources. I have not given her a name at the EFECC or the other agencies I spoke with. You're not the only person I've spoken with. Remember, I've been in Germany for weeks." Making sure Kirsten heard him, "She insists, however, that I include my conversations in my writing. I can say 'unnamed contact' of course. It's a far more compelling article if I can say that some authorities are aware of this."

They both sat in silence.

"I have a week. She wants me to give her my first story by next Wednesday, the latest. It would be better, I mean, maybe even safer for me, if I had some sort of protection. Journalism is quickly becoming a dangerous job. They get locked up in prisons. Russia likes it when people fall out of windows." Noticing Kirsten's face, "Wikipedia has a list of people associated with Russia that fall out of windows. If I could say that I've been in contact with a law enforcement agency—maybe I only have to suggest the EFECC or Europol or Interpol or even the German government knew about this crime—I might be safer."

Act Three:
April 28, 2034

Sitting in his hotel room, William typed furiously to put the final touches on his article for Andrea, his publicist. She discouraged him from being too brief or high-level. "Put everything you have into it. Don't worry about word count. I'll take care of that with the editors. We'll make it a series."

Andrea already made calls to a few media outlets and—based on her description—three well-known periodicals were preparing to make early financial commitments to the exclusive rights for the story. Andrea thought more money could be earned by selling it to multiple outlets but would see what the offers produced. Regardless, William and Andrea felt that a three- or four-part exposé series was needed. This excited potential publishers even more.

Looking through his notes, William began by outlining key trends behind the story before presenting a single plausible future. He began by quoting the source document, *China: Democracy That Works*. He pointed out that China explicitly outlined their goals and intentions to raise all of humanity out of poverty. China's expansion and drive as a founding member of the growing BRICS coalition of nations was apparent. He copied their words directly, "They intend to build a global community of shared future and presses for a new model of international relations based on mutual respect, fairness and justice, and win–win cooperation." He added other direct quotes such as, "The future of the world should rest in the hands of all peoples of the world," and "…the fruits of development should be shared by all." He then when on to argue that no one seems to ask how China might do it.

Next, William summarized the goals—and the failings—of the United Nation's decades old Millennium Development Goals and Sustainable Development Goals (SDGs). For most readers, like China's public declaration from a decade ago, this too would be new information. The article would show the "systemic apathy for the world's perpetually developing nations."

Then he transitioned into the implications of a trend to "disrupt the hegemonic status quo of global development projects that funnel money from the poorest nations of the world into the wealthiest corporations in the richest nations of the world." His writing presented the unexpected collaboration between China, Djibouti, and Yemen to build the Bridge of Horns. The bridge, he revealed, would be a key supply line on The Silk Road.

From there, William's writing turned to the novel application for Artificial Intelligence. He referred to AI as "a topic of discussion fully latent with tropian-like buzzwords and bulletized hyperbole." Without revealing his black-hatted sources, William explained in layperson's terms how HokkenStrutt's proprietary design and manufacturing techniques would likely to be "layered under ubiquitous digital artwork in such a manner that only the intended recipients would know where to find and how to separate detailed technical information free-of-charge."

Though he put off writing the last parts of the series, William hoped they would be a call-to-action by governments, regulatory bodies, and enforcement agencies around the globe. Because the laws, regulations, and ethics of AI were still being developed, understanding how it could be a threat remained only vaguely understood. His research—again shielded by phrases like 'unnamed sources,' 'documents obtained,' and 'people with

4.5 Storycasting Model: A Compelling Story

expert knowledge'—would outline for the reader that "ineffective organizational structures and the lack of expert knowledge provides adversaries a landscape of lawless opportunities to innovate at light speed."

The initial draft of the final article would include a summary of what William learned not just from his interactions with Kirsten, but from interviews with other law enforcement entities in Germany and other EU nations. Though he would not be specific, some readers might recognize departmental titles used in the article, suggesting William met with either the EFECC or Europol, and faced equal disinterest from the Federal Criminal Police Office of Germany. His writing would outline how financial crimes investigators are shackled to outdated laws and protocols.

He hoped to include polite but biting accusations that "organizations are not always structured—or have the capacity—to understand an unrealized threat or commit limited resources to something that has not happened yet. Especially one that involves multiple innovations or methods that have not been seen before. In short, they lack the ability to operationalize foresight."

A three-hour car ride from William's Berlin hotel room, Kirsten put the final touches on her report for Marlene. She felt uncomfortable. She was unsure what to include into the report and how much detail or speculation should be included, knowing that everything she knew was second-hand information. William provided her some of his initial notes and what looked to be the outline of a substantial article. She used them, heavily summarizing information without using William's more derogatory assessments. She included a brief background of William, his initial contact with Kirsten, and her first attempts to make inquiries around the EFECC.

May 15, 2034

Ironically, the same day Kirsten sent her report to her supervisor, Marlene, the first article from William Kittle was published online and picked up by other news outlets. At best, it created a mid-grade stir in some European economic circles. William referenced his interview with various companies but ended the article with a 'teaser,' stating, "Hokken-Strutt has not responded to my repeated requests for them to comment on a significant cyberattack to their digital design databases. Next week, this series will present what I've learned about this attack, that it remains unreported it as a crime, how they failed to alert their stockholders, and how it was related to China backing out of a multi-billion Euro deal with HokkenStrutt."

Somewhere in the middle of the article William made other vague references. One that put Kirsten and whomever else he'd with on edge. He wrote "While I have reached out to multiple European law enforcement bodies to propose that a novel crime is about to occure, there is no indication that the threat is being investigated or comprehended by officials. As this story continues to develop, I will present a new nexus between artificial intelligence, corporate espionage, and an effort by the Chinese government to follow through with vision that 'the fruits of development should be shared by all.' My initial investigations have revealed that the United Nations may have finally found within their member nations a government willing to eradicate systemic poverty and economic marginalization perpetuated by western nations for generations."

May 22, 2034

A week later, William's second article was released and picked up by more media outlets. He dropped more accusations and included reporting that senior leaders (to be named) within the United Nations were aligning with China as a "willing partner in achieving the Millennium Development Goals."

The same day HokkenStrutt woefully went public with the details of their earlier data breach, a reporter from Sky News conducted a live panel interview with representatives from the International Monetary Fund (IMF) and the World Bank. They publicly accused China of engaging in economic attacks. European news outlets ran wild with the story and new tangential issues arose as the IMF and the World Bank found a rising China was "inevitable but cannot be politically supported." A backlash quickly arose on social media outlets—well beyond Europe now—claiming global financial systems consistently fail to meet the needs of 80% of the world's population.

More news outlets invited leaders of multiple UN councils to chime in on the issue. Prepared statements, read in the same defiant and politically neutral tone, make it clear that the "MDGs are no longer aspirational, but with the strategies and leadership of BRICS nations a new world of human development would be on the horizon funded by something other than an economy dependent on the USD." The United States and other nations bristled with distain at the veiled threat of a new center of soft power in the world.

Inside the EFECC—who continued to remain publicly silent about the potential crime, their ambiguous authority to investigate it, and even that one of their members (technically an American on loan)—they eventually began to answer questions from Interpol. Interpol and Europol used complexly worded queries that, in plain language, ominously sounded like "What did you know? When did you know it. Who should you have told?".

May 29, 2034

On schedule, the next article from William was printed—this time with heated anticipation from media inside and outside the EU community. This third installment included information that China had already struck a deal to build the Bridge of Horns, connecting Yemen and Djibouti as a part of their Silk Road initiative. His article mapped out

4.5 Storycasting Model: A Compelling Story

long-term implications of a supply route powered by trade agreements that help the "economically strong but resource poor China" so that it no longer falls victim to trade deals unfavorable to the Yuan.

He ended the third installment with another teaser. This time he stated that he will present evidence that China will truly "share the fruits of development with the world" after they began construction on the Bridge of Horns. William promised readers that his next installment—the fourth of five—would include proof that China had a plan to share technology like HokkenStrutt's by layering technological information in AI-created images. Only intended recipients—like the current and future members of BRICS, for instance—would know where to find the images and how to de-layer the needed information. What readers didn't know, but his publisher and her editors did, was that William's interviews with multiple government agencies across Europe showed "a severe lack of coherent cyber-threat policies, ambiguous or competing authorities, and systemic lack of foresight to anticipate new crimes."

HokkenStrutt, he would show, was just the beginning of what China had planned. William's first draft of the article went on to suggest that the future of information-sharing from China to other nations using this technique would likely include technology to help poorer nations solve everything from food security issues to national power generation.

Based on the overwhelming response of the third installment of the story—and the growing information William had collected—media outlets began clamoring for interviews with William, but he resisted. Andrea agreed that he should not be interviewed until he was done with the series and was positioned to speak about—and promote—an upcoming book on the topic.

The media frenzy around William Kittle's articles continued to grow. Questions from Interpol revealed that more assertive action from EFECC could have helped the EU put political pressure on China when they backed out of the HokkenStrutt deal. The quick answer was to send Kirsten back to the US with yet another 'Warning Tag' hung around her neck while EFECC leadership continued damage control to their image and reputation within Europol and Interpol.

June 1, 2034

Kirsten's redeye from Amsterdam to Dulles landed on time at 740am. She hadn't slept a wink. Tired and filled with regret, she caught an Uber to her apartment in Arlington before heading to the office in downtown Washington DC. There, she would be summoned to a conference room to give a summary of what occurred while on loan to the EFECC, her interactions with an American journalist in Europe, and what she did not—but should have—reported back to the Treasury Department. First, however, she needed to catch her breath.

Kirsten plopped on the sofa in her apartment and opened her laptop to scan the headlines. She saw articles coming out of Germany about HokkenStrutt's stock value tanking after a cybercrime coverup. She watched small clips of interviews posted online with UN officials who praised "foresight and strategic thinking needed to advance the developing world where Bob Geldof and Quincy Jones had failed." She scanned American news outlets, caught up on the US impact of the story, and watched news reporters declare China was "confronting the US in economic warfare."

One report coming out of Amsterdam was titled "AI Stumps Interpol and Europol." She cringed, knowing this is only a taste of what she'd face in the conference room later that day. She wanted to avoid the article but turned the page and through squinted eyes saw names of senior investigators she recognized. Phrases like "necrocracy of EU forefathers" and "antiquated understanding of technological possibilities" forced her to close her laptop.

Then, as she put on her coat to head into the office, she opened her smartphone to see what showed up on her newsfeed. Morbid curiosity or a sense that she needed to be informed before facing questions, her eyes landed an article on Wired.com just released an hour earlier. The article was called "Was Kittle and his Tinfoil Hat Right About China?" The use of the past tense 'was' caught her eye. Why didn't it say "*Is* Kittle and His Tinfoil Hat…" she wondered.

She read an ominous sentence in a later paragraph. She didn't believe the words in front of her. She clicked a hyperlink leading to another headline. "Journalist William Kittle Killed in Autobahn Accident." The subtitles read "Interpol Report States His Personal Devices Missing," and "His Remaining Articles Published Post-Mortem."

Thirty minutes later, still in a haze of depression, Kirsten climbed out of a car and walked into her workplace. She took a moment in the lobby to brace herself what she assumed would be a difficult conversation with her superiors at the Treasury Department. Standing tall, she focused her mind and prepared herself to act calmly. *I have a strong resume.* She told herself. *I can be teaching back in Chicago or plenty of other universities by the beginning of the fall semester.* Heading up to the third-floor conference room, she was prepared for whatever came her way.

"Good morning, Kirsten," her supervisor began. He seemed a bit nervous as they were flanked by two other people at the large wooden table. Kirsten did not recognize them, assuming they were either from the legal department or human resources. Before she could catastrophize any longer, he continued. "I've been asked to kick this meeting off, and then once you get into the meat of the discussion, I'll excuse myself and you can continue working without me." He motioned to the two people sitting with them. "Darlene Coy and Mark Chambers are here to pull out as much valuable lessons as possible from you. They're helping define this new initiative and will act as consultants to you moving forward. By the end of the week, you'll have the first members of your team assigned to you. Things must happen quickly as we begin to allocate resources – both in the form of people and funding."

4.5 Storycasting Model: A Compelling Story

Kirsten was still trying to pivot herself out of survival mode and realize she was being relied upon to "take a lead in creating research and define future threats as they relate this initiative." Kirsten gradually pulled out a notebook and began writing as her—she now learned—*former* supervisor would ensure her a smooth transition to her new role in a new department.

"I'm not sure I completely understand," Kirsten said when he finally stopped speaking.

"Did you not get an email about all of this?" he asked cautiously. She silently shook her head that she had not. "Oh, well that's an oversight. I thought you knew." He pulled out a sheet of paper and slid it across the table.

Kirsten scanned the document quickly; aware three people were staring at the top of her head as she did. She got to the last page and skimmed a list of people that would be assigned to her team, their functional roles, and overall responsibilities. While she didn't recognize any other names, their department titles included 'Liaison to Academic Institutions,' 'Liaison to FBI and DoS,' and 'Development of Mitigations' among a few others. Finally, she saw her name. Next to it read 'Department Head: Future Threat Analysis and Research Team.' While it was clear she was not being given a promotion, she was given a job title and responsibilities that suited to her skills. More than anything, she was relieved she wasn't being fired.

She was brought back to the room by the sound of her former supervisor's voice. "I'm still working with our executive steering committee on the title. We've been thinking about Future Analysis Research Team, or Threat Analysis and Research Team." He paused and quickly exchanged a knowing smirk across the table at the other two people before he continued, "But neither choice offers an acceptable acronym."

Kirsten looked at the paper, "Yes. I see that. We'll figure that out first, I guess."

"Sorry you didn't get this information before today. You can take the rest of today to catch up on emails and get acquainted with your team. The first order of business will be for you and your team to prepare an After-Action Report. Coy and Chambers already started drafting suggestions for you, but I'd like to see a list of potential threats, capability gaps, and proposed resilience efforts within a month. The details are in an email, likely in your inbox. For now, why don't you begin with Coy and Chambers. You're an academic researcher, not an investigator. So, approach this role with that skillset. Schedule a meeting with me next week and we'll get into more details then." He stood up, shook her hand in a congratulatory manner and excused himself from the room.

Kirsten allowed the bewilderment within her diminish. Darlene introduced herself and slid a single sheet of paper across the table to Kirsten and another copy to Mark. "Last week, prior to your return to the US, I was asked to start preparing some short-term goals for us. That is, Mark and I, as your new deputies, we started to become familiar with the events that took place in Europe and prepare some recommendations for you to review."

As Darlene spoke, Kirsten nodded politely and continued examining the document she'd been handed. Along the top, were a list of summarizing paragraphs that Darlene and Mark felt were appropriate starting points for the After-Action Report Kirsten's new team would need to prepare. In the middle of the page, Kirsten's eyes landed on a list of recommended prioritized first steps. It read:

1. Define the scope and staffing needs of the [name pending] Future Threat Analysis and Research Team (FTART).
2. Create and publish mission and vision statements. Determine critical uncertainties that will drive FTART priorities for CY2035.
3. Create a timeline of events involving William Kittle and his reporting of a potential novel threat in Artificial Intelligence and his theories—founded or unfounded—on stolen proprietary technology.
4. Define the statutory gaps between AI development and US regulatory and/or law enforcement. This should include relevant knowledge from SMEs within the financial, intelligence, and investigative communities of the government.
5. With partner agencies and the UN representatives, assess the likelihood of the United Nations Security Council's alignment with BRICS nations.
6. Assess the state of AI regulations in the EU since 2024 and summarize the efficacy of AI regulations in European courts.

Mark leaned in, politely interrupting Darlene. "Kirsten, we both were very sorry to hear about the death of your friend, William Kittle. Please accept our condolences."

"Thank you." Kirsten's eyes never left the page. "Let's get to work. We need to start drafting the After-Action Report. It's only a matter of time before this happens in the US. Then it will be our turn."

The End

4.6 Grounding Storycasting with Research

I'll discuss genre later, but for now the general term *fiction* will suffice. Writing realistic fiction for strategic planning or strategic futures is unlike fiction for pure entertainment. It requires research to ensure believability and accuracy in portraying real-life situations, settings, and characters. In order to avoid inaccuracies or misrepresentations, writers engaging in Storycasting should consult reliable sources such as books, articles, or even firsthand accounts to ground the fiction in reality.

Building the previous story took some time. Whether it be delving into the details of a specific occupation (investigative journalism or financial crimes), exploring authenticities of a particular organization (EFECC's org chart), the geography of where the story takes place (Europe in general, Germany in particular) or understanding the emotional complexities of a character's experiences (an African American's experiences in Germany and a person struggling in a career she may not be ideally suited), some basic facts are essential for crafting authentic and compelling narratives that resonate with readers.

4.6 Grounding Storycasting with Research

Without changing the core ideas of the Threatcasting scenario, converting it into *Lost in Translation* took some extra research on my part.

I will not present a separate bibliography or list of references for *Lost in Translation*, but it makes the plausible more compelling when readers can get a sense of the grounding the story was built upon.

> Note: It is suggested at a minimum that practitioners gain the approval to share an anonymized copy of the original Threatcasting data prior to publishing any derivative work that used their data.

Because fiction does not require references and bibliographies, Storycasting should not either. Remember, the point here is to be compelling and engage the reader with the threat(s) and the characters, not create an academic research paper. For that reason alone, I would recommend not listing sources in either APA or MLA format but rather listing any sources of inspiration you found in an intentionally informal and informational manner. Show your effort, but not necessarily how the sausage was made. However, depending on the planned distribution or use of the final written product, it would be reasonable to have a document—either attached to the story or readily available for anyone interested—with a general statement along the lines of "This story was developed after reading more on the following topics," or "Sources used to support the ideas in this plausible future scenario included." Here's my example:

While the original Threatcasting participant's responses provided a solid premise, I reviewed the following sources for *Lost in Translation*.

- *Open-Source Intelligence Techniques.* By M. Brazzell, M.
- *Powerful Narratives. Weaponized Harmony and the Sot Power Tools of China's Rise to Global Supremacy.* Edited by J. Brown, M. Kovalsky and S. Vaughn.
- *The Occupation Thesaurus: A Writer's Guide to Jobs, Vocations, and Careers.* A. Ackerman and B. Pulisi.
- *Powerful Narratives. Weaponized Harmony and the Soft Power Tools of China's Rise to Global Primacy.* Published by The Army Cyber Institute at West Point.
- *Humanitarianism in Question. Politics, Power, Ethics.* Edited by M. Barnett and T. G. Weiss.
- *The Anthropology of Development and Globalization.* Edited by M. Edelman and A. Haugerud.
- The premise of *Three Days of the Condor.* Adapted from the book, *Book Six Days of the Condor* by J. Grady which was first published in 1974.
- *The Poorer Nations. A Possible History of the Global South.* V. Prashad.
- *The Millennium Development Goals and Beyond.* Edited by R. Wilkinson, R. and D. Hulme.

- *International Politics. Enduring Concepts and Contemporary Issues.* Edited by R.J. Art and R. Jervis.

I also reviewed the following online articles and webpages for inspiration or fact-checking:

- European Financial and Economic Crime Centre—EFECC. Link: https://www.europol.europa.eu/about-europol/european-financial-and-economic-crime-centre-efecc
- Europe's Leading Engineering Corporations. Link: https://www.scimagoir.com/rankings.php?sector=Private&country=Western+Europe&area=2200#google_vignette
- *Africa's hard road to the Millennium Development Goals.* Link: https://www.un.org/africarenewal/magazine/august-2010/africa's-hard-road-millennium-development-goals
- *World risks big misses across the Sustainable Development Goals unless measures to accelerate implementation are taken, UN warns.* Link: https://www.un.org/en/desa/world-risks-big-misses-across-sustainable-development-goals-unless-measures-accelerate
- *BRICS Countries Expand Partnership for Sustainable Development.* Link: https://sdg.iisd.org/news/brics-countries-expand-partnership-for-sustainable-development
- *Technology in Developing Economies.* Link: https://cs.stanford.edu/people/eroberts/cs181/projects/2007-08/developing-economies/
- *Closing the Technology Gap in Least Developed Countries.* Link: https://www.un.org/en/chronicle/article/closing-technology-gap-least-developed-countries

References

1. Threatcasting, pp 13–47
2. Threatcasting, Assemble the team, pp 154–158
3. State Council. The People's Republic of China (2021) China issues white paper on its democracy. Retrieved on 15 Nov 2023 from https://english.www.gov.cn/archive/whitepaper/202112/04/content_WS61aae34fc6d0df57f98e6098.html
4. United Nations Economic and Social Council (2024) Member Nations. Retrieved on 5 Apr 2024 from https://ecosoc.un.org/en/about-us/members
5. Guillen MF (2020) 2030. How today's biggest trends will collide and reshape the future of everything. St. Martin's Press, New York
6. BRICS Countries Expand Partnership for Sustainable Development. Retrieved on 5 Apr 2024 from https://sdg.iisd.org/news/brics-countries-expand-partnership-for-sustainable-development/ and https://cs.stanford.edu/people/eroberts/cs181/projects/2007-08/developing-economies/

References

7. Africa Renewal (2010, August) Africa's hard road to the millennium development goals. Sobering numbers, but some bright spots. Africa Renewal. Retrieved on 5 Apr 2024 from https://www.un.org/africarenewal/magazine/august-2010/africa%E2%80%99s-hard-road-millennium-development-goals and https://www.un.org/en/desa/world-risks-big-misses-across-sustainable-development-goals-unless-measures-accelerate
8. Threatcasting, pp 39–47
9. Threatcasting, pp 151–269
10. Threatcasting, pp 49–74
11. Threatcasting, p 52
12. Threatcasting, p 151
13. Threatcasting, p 213
14. Threatcasting, p 259
15. Threatcasting, p 53
16. Hadnagy C (2011) Social engineering. The art of human hacking. Wiley, New York, pp 176–177
17. Scott K (2017) Radical candor. St. Martin's Press, New York, p 137
18. Threatcasting, p 77
19. Yorke J (2013) Into the woods. Abrams Press, New York

Other Ways to Tell a Story   5

Futurist and author of *Future Shock*, Alvin Toffler, was referenced earlier in this book. He envisioned a future where simulated environments would offer people opportunities for escape, entertainment, education, and even work. He foresaw the emergence of virtual realities where individuals could interact, explore, and experiment without the constraints of physical reality. He suggested that technological advancements would increasingly enable people to experience simulated realities that mimic or simulate aspects of the real world. We can now partner with artificial intelligence to develop stories with us. I am not suggesting we relinquish our creativity to an inanimate object, but rather we engage in human and machine interaction. This is not just about words and thoughts either. We can leverage any number of AI tools to develop images from our text as well. As the Threatcasting methodology captures nuanced narratives and plotlines that begin with "the person" we can leverage that data from participants into a number of compelling—intellectually and visually—formats.

There are few limits here as even poetry [1] is possible. This is again and opportunity to draw others into the fray. Below are some suggestions, but I would suggest that if you returned from a Threatcasting workshop and could share the qualitative data as it appears in Figs. 4.3, 4.4, 4.5, and 4.6 to a few people and asked, "Do you want to take this and turn it into something interesting?" you might get a few creative responses. And in the process, you would be inviting a small coalition to join you in that future world with plausible threats—and the mitigations and resilience needed to thrive.

5.1 Story Length

An interesting story can be any length. Flash fiction can be anywhere from just a few sentences to a few pages. A novella falls between a short story and a novel. Typically, novellas are around 7500–20,000 words, depending on your source. George Orwell's *Animal Farm* is a good example. While novellas do not have the same intricate subplots and backstories as full-length novels, they do offer more defined conflicts than short stories. For reference, *Lost in Translation* was somewhere around 10,000 words and could be called short story.

A graphic novella is a unique narrative that blends elements of both a graphic novel—a modern interpretation of a comic book—and a novella. They present a more intricate and lengthier storyline compared to traditional comic books yet remain shorter and less extensive than a full-length graphic novel. Graphic novellas use comics-style panels with text to tell a cohesive story. They may explore a wide range of genres and themes, including fiction, non-fiction, memoir, and more. The format allows for a balance between visual

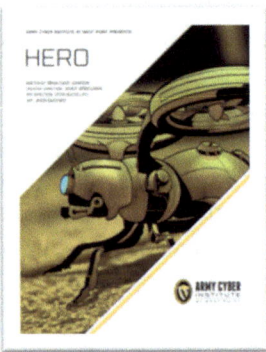

Fig. 5.1 Sample cover art of Threatcasting graphic novellas

storytelling and textual narrative, offering readers a unique and immersive reading experience. Modern graphic novellas—similar to anime, a combination of either hand-drawn art or computer-generated animation—are appreciated for their ability to convey depth of characterization, emotion, and atmosphere while also providing a visually engaging narrative.

Like many Threatcasting outputs, *Lost in Translation* would easily lend itself to this genre. I did not develop one for this book, Storycasting, however examples of Threatcasting scenarios converted into graphic novellas already exist, see Fig. 5.1. Just some of the many examples can be found here:

Dark Hammer: A Retrospective of Science Fiction Prototyping.
A PDF is available for download at:
https://threatcasting.asu.edu/Dark_Hammer_Retrospective

Hidden Stratagem—Microtargeting: The Future of Conflict. Viewable online at:
https://athena.westpoint.edu/items/6ce5d850-d413-4428-a62f-7c13e2117d9f

Hero 2028. An interactive flipbook.
Viewable online at: http://www.winkstink.com

5.2 Newspaper Front Pages

As I demonstrated earlier in this textbook, a newspaper or magazine article—in either print or digital mediums—offers an interesting option to present a potential future scenario. I say this because news—in all its forms—reflects or drives public perception about an organization, a person, an event, or all three at the same time. Not just news reporting, but even the bold catchy headlines can either influence changes in—or reinforce existing—public perceptions. For example, if a particular demographic holds negative opinions about a certain entity—for the sake of *Lost in Translation* let's consider China, HokkenStrutt, or the United Nations—news sources may prioritize negative coverage of that organization or connected events, to cater to their audience's preferences.

The investigative journalists, writers, editors, and publishers of news may choose to emphasize certain aspects of a story or downplay others based on what they believe their audience wants to hear. This selective reporting can sometimes distort the facts and prevent a more nuanced understanding of complex issues. Overall, for Storycasting, we can reflect the interconnected relationship between public perception and news coverage. By using the details from a Threatcasting scenario and presenting it as a fictitious news article from ten years in the future, we can engage in the act of storytelling. Consider how I presented the details of *Lost in Translation* in a simulated front-page format, see Fig. 5.2.

GLOBAL BALANCE
The Leading Source of Soft Power and Influence

Tuesday December 20 2034 | Issue #10

Craig McAllister

UN and China
Global Development Partners

Published by China's State Council Information Office in 2021, *China: Democracy That Works* outlines not only their model of democracy, but also their development goals for the globe and all of humanity. China's expansion in Africa and drive as a founding member of the growing BRICS coalition of nations is apparent. China intends to *"build a global community of shared future and presses for a new model of international relations based on mutual respect, fairness and justice, and win-win cooperation."* And also, their strategy *"promotes mutually beneficial exchanges and cooperation."* China contends *"The future of the world should rest in the hands of all peoples of the world. International rules should be made by all countries... ...and the fruits of development should be shared by all."*

For nearly a decade China has quietly worked to achieve their goal to empower humanity. Pundits ask, "Do you really believe they care about the world?" The United Nations, however, sees China as the answer to the question "Does anyone believe in the Millennium Development Goals?"

Above: Conceptual image of the anticipated Bridge of Horns China intends to build. Questions remain where the design originated as they fullfill their promise to connect all of humanity.

The Bridge of Horns Scandal
People's Liberation Army Base is Now a Construction Hub

After decades of dreams and failures, The Bridge of Horns will become a reality. The governments of Yemen and Djibouti are hailing the recent partnership with China as a model of future economic balances.

Skeptics, however, have fueled controversy, contempt, and conspiracies. When China built the base in Djibouti in 2017, it did so with little fanfare. Many who understand and study geopolitics, immediately noted that the base – China's first overseas military base – sat at a significant strategic point. This would be, we now know, no accident. The narrow strait between Djibouti and Yemen would be a choke point for shipping. The United States responded with equal fanfare, building Camp Lemonnier - a Naval Expeditionary base just a stone's throw from the aforementioned PLA base. Once all the powers were put in place, the real game began.

As China moves towards pre-construction planning, many wondered how the bridge would be built. The unique design requirements needed to span the strait between Yemen and Djibouti and the sandy bottom have prevented progress. Seemingly out of the blue, China found a design that works.

The proposed Bridge of Horns design may reveal China's intentions. The bridge will carry vehicular traffic, yes, but also no less than six railroad lines. Passenger trains, yes, but also how much exportation of raw materials will this provide for China's Silk Road?

Designs may have been stolen. The bridge may be an economic boon for countries at both ends. The bridge will tip the balance of global economics and soft power.

Six roads and four tracks. The Proposed Bridge of Horns will have a greater capacity for rail than roads. Analysts call the quadruple-track design a clearn indication that the bridge's intent is to facilitate the the Silk Road Initiative more than human mobility.

AI Stumps EUROPOL
Failure to Anticipate

Douglas Munro

Europol and Interpol attempt to learn the ways that AI can be used to hide virtually anything in writing and images. Laws and Policies are sure to follow, but only after expertise and perspectives are defined in strategic thinking. A call for governments to think about the threats of tomorrow leave many hoping this is a call for action.
Page 2

Was Kittle and his Tinfoil Hat Right About China?
Find out What we Know

Andrea Parker

Kittle published a book that broke down the barriers between geopolitics, global development, and East/West relations. Who is reading it? Was his fate a sign of foul play? Journalists and other investigators fear increased imprisonment and death threats become the new norm.
Page 2

HokkenStrutt Sinks
Canary in the Coal Mine?

Gilberto Pieta

Construction giant HokkenStrutt nears bankruptcy, but are they the first of many? European industrial leaders fear they are next as the world struggles to develop policies and policing of technology like AI. Who will police the 'wild west' of digitized writing now? Governments realize they are not ready.
Page 3

Fig. 5.2 Simulated front page created by the author

5.3 Internal or Organization-Specific Documents

Internal documentations, like After-Action Reports (AARs), are essential documents used in various government sectors, including law enforcement, to brief outcomes or findings, make recommendations, propose initiatives, or assess and analyze the outcomes of specific events or operations. Here, we have an opportunity to bring the story closer to the members or employees of the organization. Using the data found in Figs. 4.4, 4.5, and 4.6 a simulated internal document could be developed to present novel developments (**flags**) or potential mitigations (**gates**) presented in each plausible future scenario in—I'll say it again—a more *compelling* way. Here are some ways that the comprehensive plot and characters found in *Lost in Translation* could be presented in a more succinct way:

Simulated US Treasury Department Report. Because Kirsten was an employee of the Treasury Department, you could develop a simulated AAR or white paper based on her experiences. Start with the participant replies to the experience and enabling prompts found in Fig. 4.5: Experiential and Enabling prompts and the participant responses. You could use those datapoints and develop learning and training objectives related to the novel development of AI. As the scenario heavily involved international regulatory agencies, foreign governments, and global partnerships like the United Nations and the European Union, you could create findings that focus on the need to develop interagency coordination. Even using just the last paragraphs of *Lost in Translation*, it would be a simple task to show, not tell, the ending of the story.

Simulated EFECC Internal Report. Because of Kirsten's experience with her leadership and colleagues, a simulated internal document could be created for the European Financial and Economic Crime Centre (EFECC). To demonstrate this, I simply captured some of the information found in the participant responses related to recovery as found in Fig. 4.6: Backcasting prompts and participant responses. I generally focused on outcomes like accountability and transparency to document Europol's actions or inactions during the story. I could also have highlighted the need for policy development or revision of policies and procedures that relate, in this case, to the reporting of potential crimes, reporting to non-law enforcement or investigative employees, or an accountability system for reporting. The EFECC would act as a 'stand in' for any government or law enforcement agency represented in the stakeholders of the Threatcasting workshop.

> **NOT FOR PUBLIC RELEASE – LAW ENFORCEMENT SENSITIVE**
>
> # AFTER ACTION REPORT   AARP34-0145
>
> **EUROPEAN FINANCIAL AND ECONOMIC CRIME CENTRE (EFECC)**
> 22 Dec 2034

1. Background and Description	Pg 1
2. High-Level Requirements	Pg 2
3. Resources and Manpower	Pg 3
4. Authorities	Pg 4
5. Implications	Pg 6
6. Deliverables and Deadlines	Pg 9

1. **Background and Description**

   Based on the events of January 2034, EFECC has determined that significant errors in crime reporting occurred. Further, the widespread public perception of the EFECC (in the form of online news and pending book publication and movie release based on the same) a comprehensive review with recommendations is required. On 01 SEP 2034, an After-Action Report (AARP) process was initiated to review the EFECC's response to a report made by an American citizen of a potential crime involving HOKKENSTRUTT proprietary technology and then-unknown representatives of the Chinese Government. Within fourteen (14) days of starting, it was determined by the lead investigator that the details and implications of the incident were beyond the scope of the AARP process. On 01 Dec 2034, EFECC's leadership ordered a full-scale investigation should be made. Therefore, AARP34-0145 shall be limited to the below recommendations.

2. **High-Level Requirements**

   Details and Deadlines (Section 6) shall be developed and improved throughout the process, however, immediately upon release of AARP34-0145, internal auditors shall be assigned to separately review the following high-level requirements and provide a comprehensive list of tasks within one month of receipt.

   - Reporting procedures for EFECC non-investigative personnel who possess information about a current crime, potential new crime, or otherwise unreported criminal activity.
   - Study the current EFECC authorities to investigate crimes related to artificial intelligence, machine learning, and other new technologies used in previous crime methods.
   - Initiate a benchmarking study of European Law Enforcement entities with the goal of understanding the current and potential gaps in legal authorities to investigate crimes in non-EU member nations.
   - After a comprehensive review of policy and legal authorities, make recommendations to EFECC leadership that related to the growing economic threats of new international economic or development agreements. This should include current and future interests of the United Nations.

Fig. 5.3 Simulated after-action report for EFECC created by the author

5.4 Industry, Trade, or Academic Periodicals

Journals and reports play a crucial role in distributing relevant information and research findings within specific professional fields. Print and digitally distributed journals (many have converted to online websites) provide a platform for experts in an industry to share

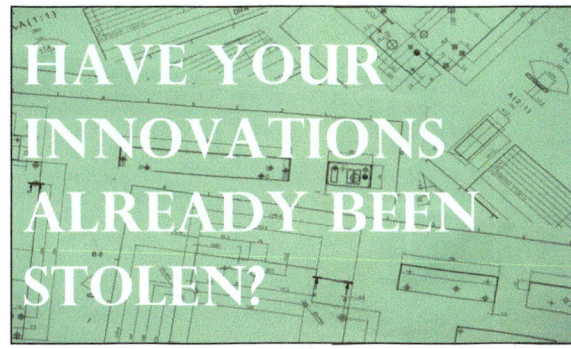

The European Journal of Infrastructure and Design

A Quarterly Publication Presented by the European Council of Manufacture and Infrastructure.

DECEMBER 2034

HAVE YOUR INNOVATIONS ALREADY BEEN STOLEN?

Investigative Journalist Uncovers Data Theft Scheme that Law Enforcement Could Not Comprehend. How will this Impact YOUR company's future?

Inside this issue we explore the following:

- The UN's Millennium Development Goals (MDGs) were once the gleaming point of hope on the horizon. However, year after year they fall short, becoming another example of the UN's irrelevance. China is seeking to develop the world equally and fairly – the whole of humanity, not just the 'first world,' - they have stated. Meanwhile the IMF, World Bank, EU, and everyone in the G7-through-G20 (who are not China) are dubious of China's intentions. Nations in agreement with *fair* global development - or in receipt of stolen technology - beg the rest of the world to ask, "Does BRICS become a 'new center of international power and influence?"

- European construction corporations like Germany's HokkenStrutt fear the hegemony of highly industrialized nations and of multi-billion-dollar infrastructure projects could be lost to BRICS nations. Further, if these projects help developing nations it stands to reason that the United Nations will increasingly turn to BRICS instead of Europe, America, and Japan to help further sticky issues like food security, global trade, and systemic poverty.

- And finally, we will discuss the unexpected collaboration between China, Djibouti, and Yemen to build the Bridge of Horns. The bridge promises to be a key supply line on The Silk Road.

Fig. 5.4 Simulated industry journal cover as created by the author

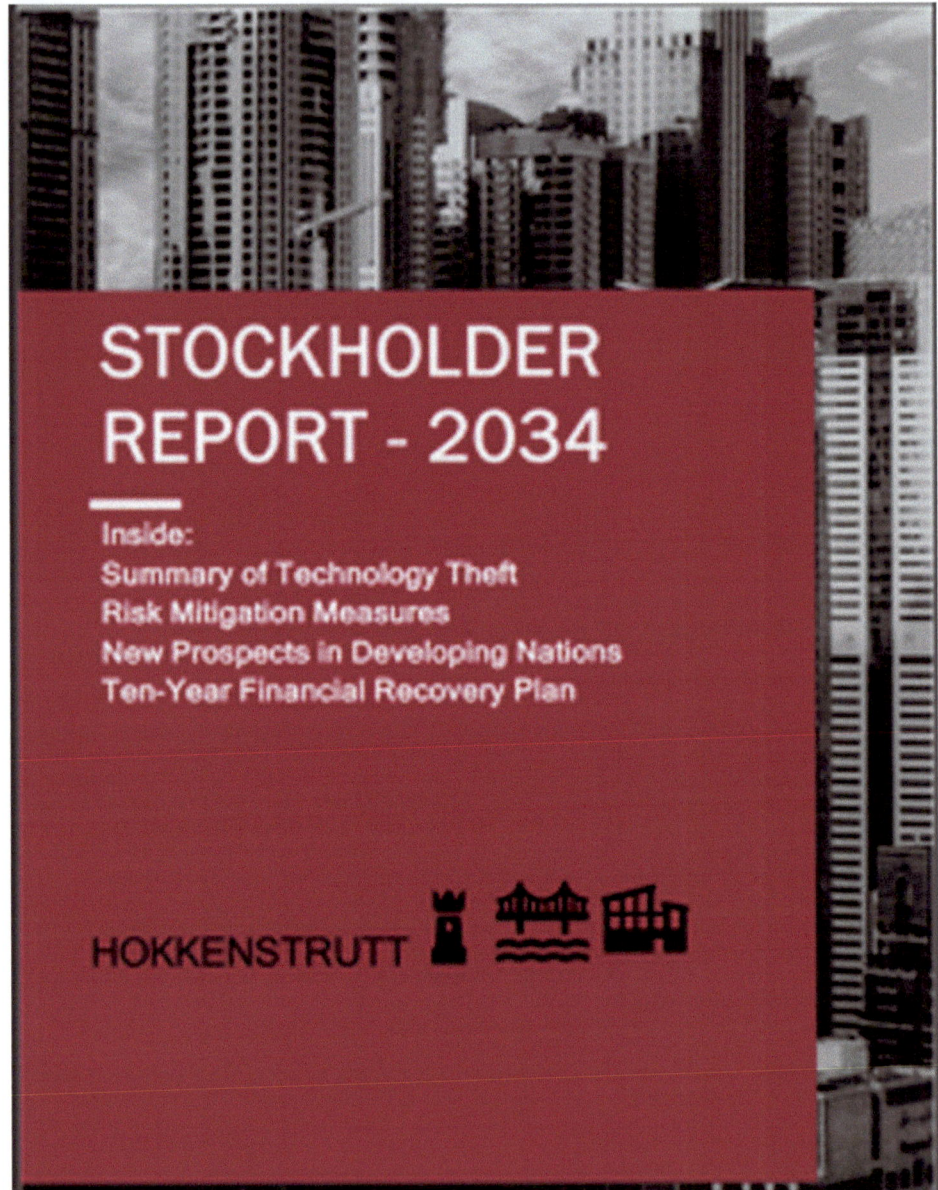

Fig. 5.5 Simulated stockholder report as created by the author

their knowledge, insights, and advancements, allowing practitioners and researchers to stay informed about the latest trends and developments. By reading industry or trade journals, professionals gain access to cutting-edge research, best practices, and case studies, which can help them enhance their knowledge and skills, stay competitive in the industry, and make informed decisions in their work. The same might apply to internal corporate reports (Fig. 5.3).

For Storycasting, we can consider academic journals in the same manner as industry journals as they are both resources for academics, students, and researchers conducting academic research in a specific field. The articles published in these types of periodicals are often peer-reviewed and backed by rigorous research methodologies, making them reliable and credible sources of information. Again, in Figs. 5.4 and 5.5, I have taken specific information from *Lost in Translation* and created covers of two simulated documents as another method of visually persuasive storytelling. Either of these could be developed into multi-page documents with the information provided.

5.5 Genre Decisions

Genre matters. Sort of. It matters in that some genres have a definite appeal to some audiences and not others. However, there may be no difference in the effort and creativity it takes to write one genre over the other. Any fiction, regardless of the many sub-genres, can be built using either one writer or with a diverse range of individuals. Do not assume that this needs to be a solitary effort. Though collaborative writing has its challenges, here too is another opportunity for human-centric design as discussed in earlier sections of this book. Consider the application of everything involved in presenting a future scenario or strategic foresight effort. This includes the source material, the reader, the writer, and the context for which you intend your broader storytelling, or Storycasting product, to be used.

One of the creators of the Threatcasting methodology, and coauthor of the book by the same name that I've referenced frequently, has a well-documented appreciation for science fiction. So much so, he authored a book called *Science Fiction Prototyping. Designing the Future with Science Fiction.* There are many historical examples of how storytelling has been used to explain science, including Robert Goddard, Hermann Oberth, and Wernher von Braun. In his book, as I am doing here, he demonstrates how to build a science fiction prototype "in five steps or less" [2], which is not unlike The Five-Act Play. For more information on sci-fi prototyping, I refer you to that book.

The article, *Science Fiction Can Still Deliver Visions of the Future*, argues that science fiction is not just dystopian reality and technological development is driven by a multitude of factors, "we see dystopia everywhere because it makes for a good story. It's the conflict, that good must triumph over bad, then humans must win over robots, and these stories are as black and white as the article itself" [3]. They do not insist the future must be all bad, however, so do not assume that any story you create from Threatcasting outputs must be dystopian. There is always an opportunity to create a happy ending. In fact, the participant replies related to recovery and resilience (gates and flags) should steer your plot to a peaceful, more optimistic future.

Speculative fiction and science fiction share a close relationship, as both genres involve the exploration of imaginative and often futuristic concepts. Threatcasting fits somewhere in this gray middle ground, I think, because they both focus on advancements in technology or common understanding of scientific principles. The boundaries between speculative fiction and science fiction are often blurred, with authors drawing upon a mix of scientific theory, philosophical ponderings, and creative world-building (Re: robust application of all the STEEPLE themes, not just two or three meeting at an intersection) to craft stories that push the boundaries of imagination while also shedding light on contemporary issues. Ultimately, both genres serve as powerful tools for envisioning possible futures and reflecting on the complexities of human existence and therefore can be leaned on for *Storycasting*.

'Useful fiction' is a relatively new term. In *Thinking the Unthinkable with Useful Fiction* August Cole and P.W. Singer describe useful fiction as "an analytic tool that melds narrative and non-fiction. Its attributes are particularly attuned to aiding in visualizing new technology and trends—key issues at play in geopolitical change emergent great power competition" [4]. Blending fiction and non-fiction as a premise for storytelling lies not in the explanation of specific breakthroughs or trends, but in shedding light on overlooked problems and systemic issues. By challenging outdated narratives of the past, this combination has the potential to bring attention to pressing issues that have been previously ignored, misunderstood, or too novel to imagine.

There are decisions to be made about how much dialogue could be used versus reliance or use of exposition. This is the seminal concept of 'show, don't tell.' The character's body language and facial expressions, for instance, help lead the reader and provide meaning to the story. Remember earlier in this book about the interpretation of the black geometric shapes and how observers interpreted non-verbal and non-human behavior to imagine them as characters. This use of human characteristics and behaviors is part of what has been called our "Like Switch." Essentially the point being that humans want and seek increased context to a story beyond what is apparent in just dialogue. In doing so it increases both the appeal and absorption of perspectives [5]. Even FBI interrogators can explain in detail how they extrapolate information from people them speaking.

5.6 Leveraging Artificial Intelligence

In just the past few years artificial intelligence (AI) has transformed the writing process. While academia and other domains are still developing basic rules of use, for *Storycasting*, it can be a helpful tool for non-writers. This is because AI-powered writing tools provide

5.6 Leveraging Artificial Intelligence

built-in grammar features and can even provide prompts for clarity and coherence. However, at the time of this textbook's writing, most Generative AI tools do not produce writing suitable for publishing fiction 'as-is' and would require editing and refinement.

Generative AI writing tools are not perfect, but in this application would be an opportunity for a creating partnership or human-machine interaction. By using AI as a writing aid, you can streamline the 'plausible-to-compelling' process. There are multiple free sources of AI-powered writing tools available. For the following demonstration, I used the website tinywow.com because it is easy to use and because all the content it creates is free for public use. Concerns arise surrounding issues such as accuracy, accountability, and ethical considerations. Issues related to plagiarism and intellectual property rights when it comes to AI-generated writing, however I am going to include in *Storycasting*, a basic demonstration by taking a small piece of information used to create *Lost in Translation* and explore how it can be interpreted by AI in different ways.

Again, below I'll show examples for demonstration purposes from a free-to-use website. Among other tools for images and graphics, it provides a number of various writing tools, including "Paragraph Writer." I also used this website because all of the material it creates is available for public use and requires no copyrite approvals. It is accessible at https://tinywow.com/write/paragraph-writer. This tool also offers the user to select a tone of voice. I did not use all of them, but it includes professional, grumpy, casual, excited, bold, secretive, and others.

I included each response below, as it was generated without any edits. You can see these paragraphs lack some of the more human nuances of writing; however they demonstrate that AI can be used to develop a basic paragraph and assist in starting the writing process. Further, because I chose various tones of voice, we can see how the same small piece of information can be represented differently to match the application or genre that best suits the medium, genre, and the intended audience or readers.

Participant questions found in Fig. 4.4 asked: "What is going on in their world? What does a day in their life look like?"

I chose the following participant response "He is beholden to his agent who promotes his work" and asked it to be converted into a series of paragraphs.

- For character dialogue, personal narrative, or an op-ed magazine article: Sarcastic.

Oh, what a joy it must be to have an agent who has all the power and control over your career. How wonderful it must feel to have someone constantly dictating what projects you should or shouldn't take, all while reaping the benefits of your hard work. I can only imagine the thrill of knowing that your success is entirely dependent on the whims and decisions of another person. Clearly, this individual's artistic integrity and personal autonomy are of no importance when they can just blindly follow whatever their agent tells them to do. It must be so fulfilling to be nothing more than a puppet on a string, dancing to the tune of their agent's demands. What a truly enviable position to be in!

For a sci-fi or contemporary fiction short story: Dramatic.

He is ensnared in a contract with his agent, bound by obligations and indebted to their influence over his career. Every decision, every opportunity, every step he takes is meticulously orchestrated and controlled by the unseen strings of the puppet master pulling at his strings. His agent dictates which projects he undertakes, where his work is promoted, and how he presents himself to the world. In this symbiotic relationship, he becomes both prisoner and benefactor, relying on his agent's guidance to navigate the cutthroat world of the entertainment industry while sacrificing a piece of himself in return. As the weight of his dependence grows heavier with each success, he grapples with the harsh reality that he may never truly be free from the shackles that bind him to his agent's whims.

For character dialogue or a news story or article written to mimic an op-ed piece: Witty.

Oh, the tangled web of art and business! Here we have a poor soul who is completely at the mercy of his agent, who holds all the cards when it comes to promoting his work. Like a puppet on strings, he dances to the tune of this powerful figure who can make or break his career with just a few well-placed phone calls or emails. But hey, that's showbiz for you! Our man may be beholden to his agent now, but who knows what the future holds? Perhaps one day he will break free from these chains and become a superstar in his own right. Or maybe he'll forever be indebted to this mysterious figure behind the scenes. Only time will tell in this dramatic tale of artistic intrigue.

For a news story, research article, or an internal report or official document: Professional.

The artist is heavily reliant on his agent, whose primary responsibility is to promote and market his work to a wider audience. The success of the artist's career often hinges on the effectiveness of his agent in securing exhibition opportunities, media coverage, and potential buyers for his artwork. The agent plays a vital role in establishing and maintaining relationships with galleries, collectors, and curators within the art world. Additionally, the agent must possess strong communication skills and a keen understanding of the industry in order to negotiate contracts, pricing, and other business arrangements on behalf of the artist. Ultimately, the artist-agent relationship is crucial for ensuring visibility, recognition, and financial stability for the artist's career.

Again, these examples might be unusable in their current state but could be leveraged to draft a paragraph or piece of dialogue, depending on your intended application. There were other options for tone of voice, and other websites would produce different outcomes but chose just the ones above to demonstrate their potential use. Also, it should be noted, that because AI tools create different replies to the same query, you can repeat the process using the same passage and tone of voice over and over until it produces a response you like best. Lastly, I should note that no AI-generated writing was used to develop the short story *Lost in Translation* and was my own original writing. I did, however, find it very useful in drafting some of the experimental writing shown in earlier sections of this textbook.

References

1. Threatcasing, p 119
2. Johnson BD (2011) Science fiction prototyping. In: Designing the future with science fiction. Morgan and Claypool, p 23
3. Priestly T (2023, December 25) Science fiction can still deliver visions of the future. Medium. Retrieved on 17 May 2024 from https://daysoffuturespassed.com/science-fiction-can-still-deliver-visions-of-the-future-32bd6df4579f
4. Cole A, Singer PW (2024) Thinking the unthinkable with useful fiction. Downloaded on 4 May 2024 from https://www.queensu.ca/psychology/sites/psycwww/files/uploaded_files/Graduate/OnlineJournal/Issue_2-Singer.pdf)
5. Schafer J, Karlins M (2015) The like switch. Simon & Schuster, New York

6

The Future of Storycasting as Viewed by the Author

I've reached the age (*That's a great way to end a book, right?*) where it can be overwhelming when I think about how rapidly things change. Not just technology, but all the letters in STEEPLE. Or how much has changed in my *short* life. But it has also taught me that today's truths might not hold up tomorrow. That's how our reality works—adapting and evolving. Repeat. It's important to stay open-minded and flexible, ready to embrace new ideas and perspectives as they come along. The future will take on new forms, challenge our beliefs, and hopefully lead us to a point in the not-so-distant horizon, not filled with unimagined threats but anticipated challenges. And in the process, we learn to let go of what no longer serves us.

Some people have "the hill they are willing to die on." Well, there was no hill. I piled up a bunch of dirt and made my own. Then I stood on top and quixotically declared to the clouds passing in the wind, "My holy and sworn enemy is a PowerPoint slide with four bullets describing our fates that shall exist whence a decade has passed. Its tyrannic dullness shall not endure within any domain I reside...." Ok, well, not that dramatic. But that's the premise.

The argument I'm making is that the robustness of strategic futures or strategic planning efforts are lost when the participant leaves the workshop, returns to their office, and their boss asks, "So what do you do at that Threatcasting workshop?" At some point, a senior leader wants to be briefed. They are busy and need to be briefed briefly. But and futures and foresight and plausible threats are very complex. Threatcasting participant cohorts, made up of subject matter experts, are consistently creating something far too complicated and nuanced and ominous for a single summary slide. At that point, all their work has been distilled down to stale breadcrumbs. So, it is little wonder why long-term strategic plans disappoint.

Just like that day off the Haitian coast, questions are my 'go-to' reaction to most new projects or imagined threats. They force me to stretch my perspectives beyond what I think I know. And I also like questions that lead to better questions. In that spirit, I'll end with a few questions and some anticipative answers. I say anticipative because today's truth will adapt to the future. Just like everything and everyone does everyday foreword.

In early 2024 when I started my literature review for *Storycasting*, I participated in some conference panel discussions. The topic was the Threatcasting methodology specifically, and futures work in general [1]. That week prompted those of us on the panel to think about how to make futures work more widely utilized as a method of building resilience to undetermined changes. How to make it more inclusive. How to build recovery and resilience measures after a community was debilitated by a cyberthreat. For me, the first question that nagged was:

What will make strategic futures outcomes more compelling? The answer to that question is not complete yet. We're still going to discover new ways to make the outcomes of Threatcasting and strategic futures more persuasive. We'll discover this through its repeated use and with every new set of workshop outcomes. The data continues to grow. There is no end point or destination. This work is like other sociological research: continual and developing and adapting. Lather, rinse, repeat. Apply, learn, improve.

I think what sets the Threatcasting model apart from others—and there are other robust and beneficial forecasting and strategic planning models out there—is it forces the entire effort down to an individual person or victim or employee. Which makes sense because workshop participants must begin by providing answers to the questions, *who is your person, what is their name, and what do they look like?*

You can do a lot of future foresight work at the discipline level. You can do it at the industry level. You can even get down to the organizational level or even a department within an organization. Using *Storycasting*, you begin with a person doing a thing in a place. That person—and any other actors in the imagined situation—is also the key to resolution and resilience. The protagonists and antagonists are the true SMEs of the story, and we rely on them to reach the desired outcomes. And they are both in the event and a part of the recovery from it. And so, the answer to the question regarding how futures and strategies can be compelling may reside in the need for people in our real organizations finding some likeness, or some affinity, or even some kinship with the person in the plausible future event. So, who is the person in your future scenario? Maybe the best answer is: Give the reader a 'future them' to relate to. We can do that through improved storytelling, or *Storycasting*.

Who will propel us into the future? I have no data to prove this, but from my observations I see the most engaged people—the ones who can most deeply envision a future—are not people my age. More often than not, the most intrigued participants, and the ones with the most daring ideas, are the ones that left college or joined the workforce in the previous five years. It would make sense that the younger generations have the most personal investment in a plausible scenario set ten years in the future. Let me say it like it is: My generation will be retired ten years after the publication of this textbook. With an innate propensity toward modernity, Millennials, Gen Z, and whomever you call 'the kids today' possess an innate ability to adapt quickly to tech-centric workplaces. With their diverse backgrounds and willingness to embrace change, the newest employees among us drive innovation and growth instead of prolonged obeyance to outmoded ideas. I want to end this with the message that I'm optimistic. Optimistic that the process I proposed in the previous pages aside, the premise behind *Storycasting* will gain traction on the softness of critical uncertainties as the newest employees of today ascend to leadership positions in the future.

I want to elicit a response in the reader. We want to get away from that painfully succinct "fact, fact, fact, next slide, forget." We want senior leaders, decision makers, and everyone to the left and right of us to react to our findings and plausible future scenarios. I want their response to be "Oh, I did not expect that." Or "That makes me nervous," which is sometimes what we hear when we read some of the detailed participant-driven scenarios. I want leaders to say "That feels realistic. I'm a little alarmed," or "Actually, we're well-positioned for that potential future threat. Better than our competitor or adversaries, in fact." I want a coworker or supervisor or subordinate to ask, "Can I see the information you used to create that? I have more questions." Or "Walk me through that again," or "How did you come to this in just a three-day workshop?"

I believe that it is possible that anyone who participates in a workshop can go back and elicit a response from their organization. In *Storycasting*, I've mapped out a few ways. I will continue experimenting with that idea. You should too. Change an article or internal report I demonstrated earlier into something more relatable to your company or industry. Try something that I haven't. I think that's what we can do better for our leaders and decision makers. If we're investing the time to build strategic futures, then we should come back with something that elicits the response from the decision maker at your organization. Because they deserve it, they should expect us to do it, and we know that they need persuasive evidence to make *informed* long-term decisions.

Reference

1. Lindsey G (2024, April 18) From bullets to belief: the power of storytelling through Sci-Fi prototypes. In: Connexions 24 conference at UT Austin. https://www.youtube.com/watch?v=akpQRC aKLjg&list=PLHeilMXzC17fsOU50t8D8J5pul2JUrVN7&index=13

Terms as Used in this Textbook

Backcasting: Working backward from a plausible future state and developing the likely steps that would lead to that state coming to fruition.

Cohort: A grouping of participants into a small, collaborative team.

Critical uncertainties: Unpredictable or unstable factors that can significantly impact a business or industry.

Competitive intelligence: The ability to gather and use information on factors that affect a company's competitive advantage.

Effect-based modeling: A system that plans and assesses strategies to outcomes by influencing related or tangential systems and capabilities.

Flags: Indicators that a future is beginning to manifest or showing actions.

Gates: Actions that can be taken to mitigate a threat as it manifests.

Novel: From Latin *novellus;* new, young, fresh, but also original and unique.

Open-ended questions: Questions that allow respondents to answer in their own words.

Open-source information or intelligence: Material or data from publicly available sources to inform or solve a specific problem.

Objectivity: The ability to see the world as it really is.

Prediction: A statement about the future that is intended to be accurate.

Scenario: A description of an alternative, possible future.

Threat: The potential for disruption, diminished opportunity, or increased risk.

Trend: A measurable change over time; historical.

Spurious relationship: A non-causal relationship between two variables.

Schema: A representation of a plan or theory in the form of an outline or model.

Stakeholders: People or groups that participate in or are affected by a program or its evaluation, such as funding agencies, policymakers, sponsors, program staff, and program participants.

Trend study: A study design in which data is collected at least two times with a new sample selected from a population each time.

If you have any concerns about our products,
you can contact us on
ProductSafety@springernature.com

In case Publisher is established outside the EU,
the EU authorized representative is:
**Springer Nature Customer Service Center GmbH
Europaplatz 3, 69115 Heidelberg, Germany**

Printed by Libri Plureos GmbH
in Hamburg, Germany